ZACK JEFFRIES

Break Through to "The End"

This book was professionally typeset on Reedsy.
Find out more at reedsy.com

Contents

Dedication   xi

How to Use This Book   1

How to use these prompts while starting your first draft or...   2

Character Arc   9

"What is this change?"   10

"Focus on the details"   11

"Hierarchy of trust"   12

"It's not what it's like"   14

"The ground"   15

"When it all changed"   16

"Big feelings"   17

"They can never know"   18

"I've got a bad feeling about this"   19

"Surprise"   20

"Pay in"   21

"Hooked on a feeling"   23

"Keep it together"   24

"You can't see it from here"   25

"Angry words"   27

"Diverging paths"   28

"Don't say it"   29

"Figure it out"   30

"Exhilaration"   32

"Easier said than done"   33
"Distraction"   34
"Don't listen"   35
"Discomfort"   37
"Be prepared"   38
"Admit it"   39
"Irksome"   40
"Future is history"   41
"I did it! Now what?"   42
"How it used to be"   44
"How did you sleep?"   45
"Mirrored failure"   46
"Mental checklist"   47
"Little by little"   49
"Forget it"   50
"Helpless"   51
"From a distance"   53
"In relation to"   54
"Holiday"   55
"You don't understand"   56
"You can't do that"   58
"Wind down"   59
"What's changed?"   60
"What if it's wrong?"   61
"What I like about you"   62
"What are they thinking?"   63
"Weight"   64
"We don't have time for that"   65
"Try and try again"   66
"This will never work"   68
"This is gonna hurt"   69

"The worst that could happen"   70

"The smell of it"   71

"The right shoes"   72

"Why it won't work"   73

"That doesn't matter anymore"   75

"Stillness"   76

"You changed"   77

"Test it out"   78

"Poker face"   79

"Temperature"   80

"Moving goalposts"   81

"Smaller or bigger"   82

"Pay attention"   83

"The downside"   84

"News to me"   85

"No regrets"   86

"Not the theme"   87

"Misunderstanding"   88

"Straight before twist"   89

Relationships   90

"I can't go on"   91

"Done differently"   92

"A harmless lie"   93

"Little annoyance"   95

"They can never know"   96

"Unmatched energy"   97

"Not my speed"   98

"Keep it together"   99

"Don't say it"   100

"Ask around"   101

"Don't give it away"   102

"Difference of opinion" 103

"Be prepared" 104

"Don't trust 'em" 105

"Admit it" 106

"Absence" 107

"I wouldn't say that" 108

"Forget it" 109

"Hierarchy of trust" 110

"You don't understand" 111

"Wind down" 113

"What if it's wrong?" 114

"What I like about you" 115

"What are they thinking?" 116

"We don't have time for that" 117

"Try and try again" 118

"Downplay" 120

"This will never work" 121

"This is gonna hurt" 122

"Why it won't work" 123

"What's unsaid" 125

"You changed" 126

"Test it out" 127

"Poker face" 128

"Misunderstanding" 129

"Reveal" 130

Plot 131

"Match the pace" 132

"The why" 133

"Don't say it" 135

"I can't go on" 136

"What does it feel like?" 137

"I've got a bad feeling about this" 138

"The ground" 139

"Surprise" 140

"I can't remember" 141

"Pay in" 142

"Keep it together" 144

"You can't see it from here" 145

"Angry words" 147

"Diverging paths" 148

"Figure it out" 149

"Exhilaration" 150

"Don't give it away" 151

"Don't listen" 152

"Discomfort" 154

"Be prepared" 155

"Absence" 156

"Irksome" 157

"How it used to be" 158

"Mirrored failure" 159

"Mental checklist" 161

"Little by little" 163

"Forget it" 164

"Hierarchy of trust" 165

"Helpless" 167

"From a distance" 168

"You don't understand" 169

"You can't do that" 171

"Wind down" 172

"We don't have time for that" 173

"Try and try again" 174

"This is gonna hurt" 176

"The worst that could happen" 177
"The inevitable" 178
"Why it won't work" 179
"What's unsaid" 181
"That doesn't matter anymore" 182
"Stillness" 183
"You changed" 184
"Test it out" 185
"Poker face" 186
"Temperature" 187
"Pay attention" 188
"News to me" 189
"Misunderstanding" 190
"Straight before twist" 191
World Building 192
"When it all changed." 193
"A harmless lie" 194
"This is completely normal" 196
"Little annoyance" 197
"They can never know" 198
"Surprise" 199
"The ground" 200
"Keep it together" 201
"You can't see it from here" 202
"Ask around" 204
"Easier said than done" 205
"Distraction" 206
"Difference of opinion" 207
"Detail in motion" 208
"Discomfort" 209
"Future is history" 210

"I wouldn't say that"   211

"How it used to be"   212

"Mirrored failure"   213

"Little by little"   215

"I can't remember"   217

"Helpless"   218

"From a distance"   219

"In relation to"   220

"Holiday"   221

"You don't understand"   222

"Wind down"   223

"What's changed?"   224

"What if it's wrong?"   225

"What I like about you"   226

"What are they thinking?"   227

"Weight"   228

"Try and try again"   229

"The worst that could happen"   231

"The smell of it"   232

"The right shoes"   233

"That doesn't matter anymore"   234

"Stillness"   235

"You changed"   236

"Poker face"   237

"Temperature"   238

"Smaller or bigger"   239

"Pay attention"   240

"The downside"   241

"Straight before twist"   242

"Reveal"   243

Theme   244

"Micro theme, macro theme" 245

"The why" 247

"Distill" 248

"What is this change?" 250

"Big feelings" 251

"A harmless lie" 252

"Keep it together" 254

"You can't see it from here" 255

"Angry words" 257

"Diverging paths" 258

"Easier said than done" 259

"Be prepared" 260

"I wouldn't say that" 261

"Hooked on a feeling" 262

"Mirrored failure" 263

"Forget it" 265

"You don't understand" 266

"You can't do that" 267

"What's changed?" 268

"What if it's wrong?" 269

"Try and try again" 270

"Why it won't work" 272

"You changed" 274

"Moving goalposts" 275

"The downside" 276

"Not the theme" 277

"Reveal" 278

Index: Glossary of Terms 279

Index: Priming the Idea Machine 283

About the Author 285

Dedication

to Jess Clapton, a great author, critique partner, and friend

to the entire #Zprompt community, anybody who ever watched the videos on TikTok

How to Use This Book

1

How to use these prompts while starting your first draft or outline

I want to help you write what you want to write. Thus, there are many ways of using these prompts:

Do you need new ideas? You could easily apply these prompts to create a new story idea. You can take any story seed you have and use the corresponding prompts to fill out an outline or zero draft. Maybe a concept for a character can be fleshed out with the character or relationship prompts. Maybe an inkling of a possible setting can grow through the world building prompts. Or maybe you have a cool idea for a story's climax and can use the plot prompts.

If you do not already have a story seed, then you can use a writing exercise I call "priming the idea machine" in the index.

What if you already have a story you're working on? GREAT! If you're stuck anywhere in your story, I'm hoping that you can apply any of these prompts to your work! So start wherever you like.

How to use these prompts while writing your first draft

In theory, this is the easiest way to use these prompts. Consider them a safety net, something you don't have to use for every writing session, but a precaution that's there for the times the words aren't coming as easily.

Here's what I suggest—When you don't feel like writing, try to identify what's missing from this scene as far as the major aspects listed in this book (Character Arc, Relationship, Plot, World Building, Theme). If one of these pillars of your story is weakest in your scene, you can focus on building that up. And I find when I'm focused on something small and controllable, I tend to get overwhelmed less. This is how I overcome the dreaded "writer's block."

So please don't feel you have to use one of these prompts for every writing session; that's more pressure on your creativity, and that's what can cause anxiety, stress, and blockage. If you learn nothing else from this book, please realize that pressure and expectations are what slows writing momentum. If you remove those, you can return to the fun and freedom of writing. That's what these prompts are here to help you do.

How to use these prompts while revising

Already finished your story? I've got great news for you! I designed all of these prompts to work as inspiration for something new as well as another approach to something you're already written.

As many of us know, rewrites are really what crafts the story.

3

The first draft was just the bones, just the idea, just a rough sketch. Revisions shape the story into something compelling for your reader.

To use these prompts in revisions, it's best to understand what the weakest element of your current scene or manuscript is. Maybe you've got alpha or beta readers, or maybe you just have things you've noticed and you want to work on. You can strengthen these elements individually by working the separate prompts:

Character Arc
Relationships
Plot
World Building
Theme

My phrasing

These prompts have been transcribed from my Tiktok account. I've revised them and passed them through beta readers and editors. But the tone and word choice is still conversational. This is my voice talking to you, trying to help.

That means I use words like "oftentimes" and asides in parentheses. This is how I talk. I figured this would be easier to follow than perfect grammar with a distant instructional tone. I'm not here to instruct you. I'm here to talk to you about writing prompts I thought up that can hopefully help.

If you run into a sentence that doesn't make sense, I recommend reading it aloud. It may need read on paper like a normal story craft nonfiction book, but it should sound like a person talking with you.

My favorites and priorities

Speaking generally, I put the aspects and prompts in order of importance. That's not to say that the deep cuts aren't helpful, I simply tried to front load each set of prompts with the ones with the most potential to be helpful to a broad target of manuscripts.

What is #ZPrompt

I love the *concept* of writing prompts (even though I thought I hated them in practice), especially as tools to break out of writer's block.

There are plenty of theories about writer's block- from fear of success, to psychological trauma. There are some folks who don't believe writer's block is real. There are others who believe that writer's block separates hobbyists from professionals.

I personally believe that we are all different people bringing our own experiences, mental states, and circumstances to our writing. I'm not a "write every single day" kind of writer, and often, I find myself drifting through multiple days of not writing. I believe writer's block exist. And for me, what helps break my non-writing streaks is taking pressure off myself. If I'm focused too much on character or adhering to the plot I've thought up, then that self-imposed pressure might keep me away from my laptop. So I've found that focusing on specific aspects of what I'm writing gives me permission not to focus on big, intimidating aspects of my work-in-progress. If I can put my energy into approaching the scene I'm stuck on from a different angle, it removes that pressure.

I've been in many forms of writer's groups. One of the most successful one I've been a part of started every meeting with a 10-minute free-write based on a prompt. The problem was, I always tried to pivot every prompt to add words to my current work-in-progress. If I was in the midst of large format story-telling, writing and putting my creativity towards words I couldn't use within that current book felt like a waste to me. That became a source of anxiety for me. Or if I did write something from the prompt, I felt guilty.

So when I formed my own writer's group, I began to give prompts that were nontraditional, allowing the writer to apply the prompt to current works-in-progress. For example, I loved prompts based on film camera movements. By approaching a scene as a zoom in, zoom out, or slow pan, my writing opened up to richer descriptions and allowed the writers present to apply prompts to their current projects.

Fast-forward to me attempting to create Tiktok content that I could make consistently over a long period, I revisited the idea of prompts that writers can use to break any blocks without "wasting" any words. And #ZPrompt is an original hashtag I created so I could find the videos easily.

I start almost all of my #Zprompt videos, I've got a writing prompt for you! I don't like traditional writing prompts where I come up with an idea and expect you to write about it, I figure you're a writer, you've probably got tons of ideas.

How the prompts are structured

So all of these prompts are based on my TikTok videos using the hashtag #Zprompt. Here's the structure of those:

INTRO I've got a writing prompt for you. Author Z, Zack, or Zachary Jeffries here. I don't like traditional writing prompts where I come up with an idea and expect you to write about it; I figure you're a writer, you've probably got tons of ideas.

NAME This prompt is called (name of prompt). Feel free to favorite this and come back to it.

OBSERVATION I make an observation about commonalities of well-written stories, or real life

PROMPT So what would happen in your current or next scene if your main character or perspective character (insert the point of the prompt)

IMPLICATIONS Three questions concerning ways the prompt could enrich your story based on Character arcs, Relationships, Theme, world building, Plot

In this book, I'm not repeating my opening line for every single prompt. I've also added a resource at the end of each prompt, allowing you to easily see how the same prompt can be used to help multiple elements of your story.

So why are they structured like that?

By starting with an observation about well-written stories or even real life, I'm hoping the prompt will help your reader connect with your work, either in relatability or realism.

By making the prompt a question, you still have the freedom of doing whatever you want in your scene with your characters! You're in control. My question is simply "What would happen if..." I hope that question sparks your creativity and leads you to discover a new aspect of your story. You don't have to try the prompt. You can use the idea in any form to help write your story. I'm just hoping that the prompt will give you a new angle and relieve you of any blockage preventing you from writing the best story you can.

The implications are really the meat of improving your writing craft. I designed these questions to force you to look at different ways of strengthening these core aspects of a story. You'll find that MANY of the prompts repeat for different aspects throughout this book. What differs between each of them is the implications of applying the prompt. The same prompt can strengthen more than one aspect, for example, the theme and the character arcs. And the best use of these prompts will strengthen multiple aspects of your work at the same time.

Character Arc

A character's arc is their internal journey of change throughout the story, contrasting with the external actions that make up the plot. Typically, characters evolve to become smarter, more emotionally intelligent, more moral, less moral, or amoral. To ensure a character's change feels gradual and believable, it's crucial to track their progress throughout the story.

One helpful exercise is to break the character arc into five beats, representing five distinct actions or thought processes at different points in the story. These beats demonstrate the character's descent or ascent along their arc.

"What is this change?"

All the time in the world around us, things are constantly changing, but especially in stories. Otherwise, there would be no story, and all conditions would be completely stagnant. Things are changing in your story.

What would happen in your current or next scene if your main or perspective character sensed a change that they didn't understand?

Can you reveal more about the character by showing how they would react to this change that they are uncertain of? Can you foreshadow what is going to happen to your character? Can you create dramatic irony by letting the reader know what's happening but the perspective character doesn't get it?

Use this prompt for theme.

"Focus on the details"

Sometimes when we're in the middle of doing something that's incredibly hard, we need our brain to focus on something simple to get through it. Like when I did long distance rides on my bike, I would literally focus on one part of my handlebars and I would kind of zone out and it would make the tougher parts go by easier.

What would happen in your current or next scene if your main or perspective character focused on a tiny detail while overcoming a difficult act?

Can you use this opportunity to string out the tension? Can this tiny detail emotionally resonate with your character and reader? Can this be a moment of calm in the middle of a lot of difficulty or high stress?

"Hierarchy of trust"

Peaple trust in different ways to different degrees. Sometimes you don't trust someone you know to be honest, but you feel like you know them well enough that you know what they're going to do, despite what they say. You trust your knowledge of them. There are people who fill certain roles in your life that you might not trust as much as that role would traditionally dictate a friend or sibling that you know you really can't depend on. Someone that is in the outer edges of your friend circle, that you just trust implicitly.

What would happen in your current or next scene if your main or perspective character said or did something that changed the hierarchy of trust? So that one character that was trusted to some degree is now trusted more or trusted less?

Is this a way to let the audience in on your character's values, or how those values are shifting? Can this demonstrate growth or frustration? Can this change in trust influence later decisions the character makes?

Use this prompt for relationships.

Use the prompt for plot.

"It's not what it's like"

Most people can't help but look through the lens of our emotions at the world around us. And that sometimes means that if we're in a bad mood, something that is beautiful will appear less beautiful to us, or, when in a great mood, something that is gross appears less gross to us.

What would happen in your current or next scene, if you juxtaposed your perspective character's emotion with what they were experiencing? Their heightened emotion made them perceive something differently than they normally would.

Is this an opportunity for comedy? Can you really just drive home how much that emotion is affecting them right now? Can you create tension since some of the other characters won't understand this emotion but the reader will be completely cognizant of how emotional that character is at that moment?

"The ground"

Most people, as they move through their life, their day, or any space, have a surface underneath them. Something they walk on, something they roll on, something that they move along, whether it's floor, a walkway, or the ground.

What would happen in your current or next scene if you added a detail about the ground that in some way, shape or form affected the story?

Can the character have a strong opinion about the ground? Will the character's relationship with the ground change over the course of their journey? Can the character taking the ground for granted become an obstacle?

Use this prompt for plot.
   Use this prompt for world building.

"When it all changed"

Almost all of us are different than we were when we were younger. And for many of us, there is a specific point in time in which our worldview or our ideas about the nature of humanity changed.

What would happen in your current or next scene if your main or perspective character juxtaposed what they would have thought of a situation before and after their worldview changed?

Will this help explain why your main character is the way they are? Will this make your main character appear more mature or farther along in their arc? Will this connect your reader to your character?

Use this prompt for world building.

"Big feelings"

I think one of the most difficult aspects of "show, don't tell" is when it comes to feelings and reactions and emotions. Not blatantly using the word sad, happy, surprised, but unpacking what that feels like to experience those.

What would happen in your current or next scene, if you took the biggest emotion experienced by your main or perspective character and unpack it without using that word?

Can you relate the feeling to a previous time that character felt the feeling? Can you expand the concept of the feeling so the character's emotion drives the scene? Will your character feel differently at different moments in their arc?

Use this prompt for theme.

"They can never know"

I really love the dramatic irony of knowing what's going on inside a character's head versus what's going on externally in the scene. People's opinions of other people, the perspective character's opinion of the characters that they interact with, and how that differs in their head from how they actually act.

What would happen in your current or next scene if your main or perspective character had a very strong opinion about another character that was not revealed through their interaction?

Can you manage to characterize both the perspective character and the other character for the reader? Can the character's opinion change throughout the story to demonstrate growth? Or maybe you just create comedy by having a perspective character bite their tongue about how they really feel?

Use this prompt for relationships.
  Use this prompt for world building.

"I've got a bad feeling about this"

Going into every scene, characters have something in mind about what's going to happen just like we do in real life. We intend to talk to our boss about a raise, we intend to talk to our partner about our day, we intend to talk to our dog about getting a treat.

What would happen in your current or next scene if your main or perspective character had a bad feeling about what's going to happen next?

Can your character's pessimism help track where they are on their arc? Can you show the reader how pessimistic or optimistic your character normally is?

Use this prompt for plot.

"Surprise"

I don't know about you, but in my everyday life, I'm constantly surprised by things; mostly because I have a four- year-old daughter, but also because the world is an amazing place and things are constantly happening, and I don't know it all.

What would happen in your current or next scene if your main or perspective character was surprised by something?

Will it make the character more realistic to your reader? Can you track your character's arc by showing their expectations? Will the type of action that surprises your character change throughout your story?

Use this prompt for plot.
   Use this prompt for world building.

"Pay in"

So, every single well-crafted story has payoffs. Around the end, there are things that come back which have been alluded to. These payoffs achieve emotional impact because the reader has an expectation, then they happen or they don't happen. Either way, readers are finally given some sort of closure. Now, the only way for these things to emotionally resonate is if the readers have an opinion of the payoff happening (they want these things to happen, or not to happen or afraid they're going to happen or afraid they're not gonna happen). That means just starting in motion this idea that something might or might not happen is not enough. You have to continually allude to it; you have to pay in so it pays off in the end.

In your current next scene, how can you pay into an idea that has nothing to do with the scene, but has everything to do with a payoff that's happening later?

Maybe you can show the reader that it's still on your perspective character's mind. Maybe you can remind the reader what importance this thing has to your character arc. You can even juxtapose it for your reader by showing how little it matters to the characters, but reminding the reader how much it matters to them.

<u>Use this prompt for plot.</u>

"Hooked on a feeling"

Oftentimes as writers, when we are describing feelings, the difficulty of the description or the depth of the feeling to the character determines how much time and how many words we spent describing that feeling. If it's really tough to describe a feeling, it can take more words, it can really hit the character harder, we're going to take more words. However, whatever we take the most words to do is what the reader will take as most important to them.

What would happen in your current, next, or last scene, if you expanded the feelings of the main or perspective character that you as the writer thought was the most important for the reader to understand. Unpack those feelings so that it took more words in any other feelings you described in the scene.

Is this an opportunity for foreshadowing? Can you strengthen the connection between the reader and that character? Can you check in with your character's feelings to establish where they are in their arc?

Use this prompt for theme.

"Keep it together"

S o I imagine in your story, that characters are going to go through some stuff: ideas, emotions, etc. Things are going to hit them to give them a big reaction.

What would happen in your current or next scene if your main or perspective character was trying to keep their reaction to themselves?

Can you string tension throughout it to make the reader wonder if the person is going to be able to keep it together and keep their mouth shut? Can you add depth to why the thing matters so much to that character by getting their inner dialogue going? Can you reinforce the importance of the entire character arc by focusing on how this character is going to keep it together and not reveal what matters so much to them?

Use this prompt for relationships.
Use this prompt for plot.
Use this prompt for world building.
Use this prompt for theme.

"You can't see it from here"

The world around us affects how we perceive the world around us. If I am looking through a window outside in that window is dirty, then that affects how I see the world outside. Or, looking at someone but the light is in my eye, that affects how I look at that person. My hair going across my glasses affects how I see things. Is there a way in your story that the setting, the world around, the perspective character or the main character can affect how they perceive things? Maybe in a literal sense, maybe not in a literal sense, maybe by way of their socio-economic status, employment status, relationship with their house.

What would happen in your current or next scene if your main or perspective character realized and focused on how much the world around them is affecting how they perceive things?

Will that level up your main character on their quest for what- ever their character arc is? Can you demonstrate how your character physically changes over the course of the story? Can you show how their worldview shifts?

<u>Use this prompt for plot.</u>
  <u>Use this prompt for world building.</u>
  <u>Use this prompt for theme.</u>

"Angry words"

Mood is the emotional atmosphere of a scene. In movies, they'll use camera tricks and lighting, literally, where they placed the camera and how it looks at the character and sometimes other effects like fog, to establish mood.

But in writing, we have our words, we have the prose, a great way to establish mood is your diction.

What would happen in your current or next scene if you chose your words to reinforce the atmosphere of the scene or the mood of the main or perspective character?

Can you increase the gravity of a moment important to your character? Can you reveal some nuance about your character? Is this an opportunity to describe the same object in two different moods to show character growth?

Use this prompt for plot.
  Use this prompt for theme.

"Diverging paths"

I n life, and probably in your story, people, characters have choices. Maybe this is a choice of two things between two paths to take. Maybe it's more than that.

What would happen in your current or next scene if your main or perspective character had to decide between two things and thought about what the future would be like with either choice?

Is this an opportunity to demonstrate your character's imagination? Can you foreshadow what's going to happen to them later in the story? Is this a way to check in on a thought process of your character that will change as the story develops?

Use this prompt for plot.
  Use this prompt for theme.

"Don't say it"

I love dramatic irony, where there is a gap of knowledge between what's going on between the characters and what the characters know and what the reader knows.

What would happen in your current or next scene if your main or perspective character said the opposite of what they were thinking or feeling? I'm talking about the direct opposite. I'm talking about, "I hate this person..." and then they say, "I love you."

Will that make your characters feel real and more relatable? Can the character lie about something that they'd act differently about later in the story? Can you reveal to the reader a personal reason why the character is lying?

<u>Use this prompt for relationships.</u>
  <u>Use this prompt for plot.</u>

29

"Figure it out"

Someone smarter than me once said that every book is a mystery to the reader. After all, the reader is figuring out every aspect of the story as they go along, unlocking a mystery of what it's about and what the characters are doing and why they're doing it. But the truth is, every scene that your character walks into is a mystery. And they are figuring things out. They're figuring out what's going on, and they're gleaning new information.

What would happen in your current or next scene, if you focused on how the main or perspective character got new information and figured things out?

Will it add tension as there's a limited amount of time for your perspective character to figure this out? Maybe you can flex your mystery writing skills and throw some red herrings in there maybe just to confuse the main character or to add a more complete picture of what's going on in the scene. Is this an opportunity to let the reader into the perspective character's head and see what details they notice? In what order?

Use this prompt for plot.

"Exhilaration"

After doing something incredibly physically demanding, some- thing that seemed impossible, or even something as simple as solving a riddle, you get this little hit of serotonin. You get some adrenaline. You get exhilarated.

What would happen in your current or next scene if your main or perspective character was exhilarated, but they had to power through that to work on the next thing, to do the next thing, to solve the next problem?

Will this present an obstacle for them? Is this a way to catch your character off guard? Will this help characterize how they deal with pressure?

Use this prompt for plot.

"Easier said than done"

Oftentimes, we can talk a big game about an action that is harder than we expected. Or sometimes we bluster on purpose to show off.

What would happen in your current or next scene if your main or perspective character had to complete some action based on a declaration they had made earlier? It doesn't have to be as big as independence or bankruptcy, it can be simply saying, "I am going to do this." Once they get to that point, now their actions associated with it that maybe they did or did not foresee.

Is this a chance to show where your character is on their arc? Can you show how realistic, pessimistic, or naïve the character is at that point in the story?

Use this prompt for world building.
  Use this prompt for theme.

"Distraction"

The world is constantly moving around us, things keep going, no matter how focused we are, no matter how singularly important our goal is.

What would happen in your current or next scene if your main or perspective character had a difficult time looking through the distractions and focusing on their objective or goal?

Is this a way to show the reader how important the goal is to the character? Is this a way to let the reader know where they are on their arc? Can this show the character or reader that their original goal isn't actually that important?

<u>Use this prompt for world building.</u>

"Don't listen"

One big thing that being a dad has taught me is, it is difficult for kids to think about what they're doing while they're doing it because they just are so excited about doing it. And that makes sense because that's not just exclusive to kids. Oftentimes as adults, while we're doing something that is important to us we forget everything that we're supposed to remember and we just do it.

What would happen in your current or next scene if your main or perspective character was doing something the wrong way because they were not thinking about the steps that they need to take while they did it?

They realized that they were doing things the wrong way and that they were not taking the correct steps and they still couldn't correct it while they were doing the thing.

Will this garner empathy from your readers? Can the detail they don't remember come back later in the story to show growth?

Use this prompt for plot.

36

"Discomfort"

In most societies we are encumbered with things that we wear, as well as hair, sometimes glasses, sometimes contacts, all of these things have the potential to give us physical discomfort.

What would happen in your current or next scene if your main or perspective character actively worked against a physical discomfort as they moved through the scene?

Can this discomfort represent what they're feeling emotionally at that point? Can the character act differently about the same discomfort at different points in the story?

Use this prompt for plot.
  Use this prompt for world building.

"Be prepared"

Chances are your characters are preparing or planning for something... Maybe something that is related in some way, shape or form to the climax of your story.

What would happen in your current or next scene if your main or perspective character actively prepared for something coming later, in the midst of something happening now?

Is this an opportunity to show how your character thinks? Can you show the audience their priorities at this stage in their arc? Would their preparation change depending on the point in their character arc?

Use this prompt for relationships.
 Use this prompt for plot.
 Use this prompt for theme.

38

"Admit it"

We all make all kinds of admissions. Every single day with almost everyone we interact with. Moments of us being vulnerable enough to tell the truth, no matter how important or unimportant, that information is.

What would happen in your current or next scene if your main or perspective character admitted something to another character they were not planning to admit?

Can you use this to surprise your audience? Is that an opportunity for a big character growth moment? What made this character admit something at that moment?

Use this prompt for relationships.

"Irksome"

There's a lot of things that might get under our skin. There are things that we might dislike, there are preferences, pet peeves, but sometimes, there are things that we don't like, and we can't explain why we don't like them.

What would happen in your current or next scene if your main or perspective character ran into something that annoyed them, but they couldn't put their finger on it.

Can this color your character? Can this better reflect the mood of the scene? Can your character be bothered by something in the beginning of the story that would slide later on, or vice versa?

Use this prompt for plot.

"Future is history"

Sometimes it's difficult to see, but everything happening around us is happening in a time period that will one day be history. Seeing the context of where this time period will fit and what it will be looked back upon as and what it will lead to is often difficult.

What would happen in your current or next scene if your main or perspective character thought about how their current time period will be looked upon in the future? And this doesn't just apply to history-changing events, or giant plots that affect a lot of people. They can just look at the time period and think how will people look back on this?

Will this show how immature or mature your perspective character's worldview is? Can this show how the character changes?

Use this prompt for plot.

"I did it! Now what?"

In books, there's going to be a climax (hopefully). And at that climax, there will be a feeling of accomplishment and/or failure, things will change and characters will feel a big way about themselves and what is happening. But what about all the landmarks on the way?

In life, it's about the journey, not the destination. There is no singular climax in which the story is over in life. You reach these certain landmarks and you keep going. And oftentimes, a landmark that seems like a big deal when it's far away, or even as you're approaching it. After you complete it, then you're like, "Now what?"

What would happen in your current or next scene if your main or perspective character achieved something, reached a landmark, hit a status that they didn't really think they were going to, but their story is not over yet?

Will the character have to find new motivation to continue on their arc and journey? Will that goalpost just move further away and string along tension toward the next goal? Is this an opportunity to delve deep in their emotions and make them more realistic and relatable to your reader?

"How it used to be"

As I get older and slowly turn into my parents, one thing that I notice that I do all the time is talk about how things are different. As I drive around, I'm like, "Oh, that used to be a grocery store," or "that building is going up fast" or "I remember when this used to be farmland," and all of that really boring old people stuff. What would happen in your current or next scene if your main or perspective character focused on a change that they noticed in their setting or characters around them?

Could that show maturity in your perspective character? Can the change in the setting mirror changes in your character? Would your character notice change differently at different points in the story?

Use this prompt for plot.
  Use this prompt for world building.

"How did you sleep?"

Thanks to modern medicine, we understand now that how we sleep really affects how we live the next day. Sleep affects not only energy levels, but how fast we can process information or even how well we can remember new information.

What would happen in your current or next scene if your main or perspective character reflected on how they slept, and then realized how that affected their actions as they move through the scene?

Can this physical detail make your character more realistic to the reader? Can this demonstrate everything they've been through so far in this book? Is this a chance for their actions not to match up to their competence?

"Mirrored failure"

A big obstacle when writing a book is making sure that your main character is staying active. Passive characters can be unrelatable and cause the reader to dislike them or lose interest in your story. You can really bog your whole book down. Some traps that can cause passive characters are flashbacks, observing, and long descriptions. If they're not directly related to an active scene or an action, such traps can slow reader momentum or even bore them into putting the story down.

What would happen in your current or next scene if your main or perspective character remembered a time they acted and failed as it related to an action in the present scene?

Will this make your character appear more endearing to the reader? Is this a way to fill out the character's backstory? Can this show how the character has changed?

Use this prompt for plot.
   Use this prompt for world building.
   Use this prompt for theme.

"Mental checklist"

Now, I don't know about you guys, but I go through mental checklists all the time, and not just when I'm doing something big and important. But also like, every time I leave a place, every time I go to drive someplace, I'm going through a lit of what I need- wallet, phone, keys, and probably a snack just in case.

As an author, I do a lot of in-person events. And for those in-person events, I'm often doing a mental checklist and often realizing that I forgot something.

What would happen in your current or next scene if your main or perspective character was preparing to do something (it doesn't have to be a big thing), and as they're doing a mental checklist, they realized they'd forgotten something? Then, they had to determine how important that thing was.

Can this further characterize them? Will their reaction to a self-created obstacle differ depending on where they are within their arc? Will they conquer this obstacle, or perhaps realize they didn't need the item in the first place?

Use this prompt for plot.

"Little by little"

Unless you're writing a pretty short story, your characters are probably going to have to go through a lot of steps toward their goal. Whether or not they achieve that goal, there are going to be many steps along the way. Oftentimes, when we're focused on the goals, these tiny steps that we take seem too small for our patience, seem like we're not making progress, and seem like the goal is that much further away.

What would happen in your current or next scene if your main or perspective character started getting frustrated with the very small amount of progress that they're making towards an overarching goal?

Can this be an opportunity to show how they deal with frustration? Can you relate their journey toward their goal to their journey as a character? Can you revisit this frustration throughout the story to show growth?

Use this prompt for plot.
  Use this prompt for world building.

"Forget it"

I don't know about you, but I'm always forgetting stuff. I know I'm old, but like, there's just too much stuff to remember in life.

What would happen in your current or next scene, if while your characters were actively doing something, you reminded the reader of something that that character was forgetting?

Can this dramatic irony produce comedy? Is this an opportunity to show the reader where the character is on their arc? Can the way the character comes to notice their forgetfulness reflect their arc?

Use this prompt for relationships.
    Use this prompt for plot.
    Use this prompt for theme.

"Helpless"

One thing that I like to focus on as a person is controlling my controllables and understanding what is out of my control. And that's a pretty simple thing to say, but not a simple thing to do. There are things that are always out of our control, that can frustrate us, that can get in our way, that can ruin our plans. These things can sometimes seem in our control when they're not, or vice versa.

What would happen in your current or next scene if your main or perspective character focused on what was out of their control?

*Be careful with this prompt because you don't want your main character to be passive.

Is this an opportunity to show how their mind works? Is this a way to show where they are in their character arc? Will they gain a better or worse understanding of controllables as the story moves forward?

Use this prompt for plot.

Use this prompt for world building.

"From a distance"

I f your story has a deep perspective, either first person or close third person, then you cannot step out of that character to look at anything. But, your character can guess or think about what things look like from afar.

What would happen in your current or next scene if your main or perspective character took a distant look at the situation that they were in? This could mean literal or figurative. Just a look at what the actions they are involved in look like from afar.

Can this give a glimpse into how your character's mind works? Will your character have a realistic or dramatized concept of what they look like from afar? Is your character's concept of how they look an indication of the personal journey they're on?

Use this prompt for plot.
  Use this prompt for world building.

"In relation to"

When describing scenery, or anything physical to be honest, it's easy to just describe it at face value, or even go a step forward and imbue the description with the emotion of the character.

What would happen in your current or next scene, if you described anything physical in terms of how it helps the character reach their next and most immediate goal?

Is this a way of keeping your character active? Can this demonstrate your character's focus? Would your character utilize their surroundings differently in different moments in the story?

Use this prompt for world building.

"Holiday"

Unless the world of your story is vastly different from our own, then there are anniversaries, birthdays, and holidays that take place. And as you may or may not know, almost every single day has some sort of assigned significance to it, whether it commemorates a person, an action or an idea.

What would happen in your current or next scene, if it took place during a holiday specific to the world of your book?

Can this holiday have a different meaning internally for your main character or perspective character than it does for everyone else? Can you reveal your character by showing their attitude about this holiday? Will your character's reaction to the holiday demonstrate their emotional state?

Use this prompt for world building.

"You don't understand"

Whether we are neurotypical or neurodivergent, it's not always easy to communicate what we are thinking to other people.

It's very difficult to get somebody to see through our own perspective, no matter how good we are with words, no matter how well we know the other person, no matter how well we understand the social cues that we share with our audience.

What would happen in your current or next scene if your main or perspective character was having a difficult time explaining a thought to another character and had to keep changing tactics?

Will this make this character more relatable? Can you show where the character is in their emotional journey by showing them get frustrated? What would change about this dialogue at different points in your character's arc?

Use this prompt for relationships.
  Use this prompt for plot.

Use this prompt for world building.
Use this prompt for theme.

"You can't do that"

Satisfying character arcs are the ones that finish with the main character doing something that seemed absolutely impossible for them to do. And I'm not talking about a superhuman feat. I'm talking about something that internally, you wouldn't think that the character was capable of because of trauma or emotions. They come to admit that they needed help, or for them to trust someone else.

What would happen in your current or next scene if your main or perspective character alluded to not being able to do the one thing that you know that they're going to have to do in the climax? If you just reinforced that there's no way that this character is going to be able to do that?

Is this a way to track where your character is on their arc? How does the character currently feel about their inability to do this task? Will their opinion of the task or their ability change along their arc?

Use this prompt for plot.
  Use this prompt for theme.

"Wind down"

Whether it's physical or emotional, there should be some action in your story. But whenever we encounter action in our everyday lives, there is a bit of wind down afterward, moments of our mind and body trying to return to normal, but sometimes that wind down can get in the way of us wanting to do something else, to immediately start another action. Sometimes it scrambles the brain a little bit so we can't think straight for the next thing.

What would happen in your current or next scene if your main or perspective character's body or mind was winding down and became an obstacle for what they wanted to do next?

Is this a chance to explore a character flaw? Will this test the character's patience? Does the character currently have the ability to recuperate before taking on another obstacle?

Use this prompt for relationships.
  Use this prompt for plot.
  Use this prompt for world building.

59

"What's changed?"

Oftentimes as we get older, we learn more context about the world around us and understand things more. We can see the same piece of information, memory, or object and understand it better. We have learned, we have grown, we just get the context more than we did the first time that we encountered it.

What would happen in your current or next scene if your main or perspective character revisited a memory, an object, or an idea with a new context and realized that there was an added meaning or a different meaning entirely?

Can this demonstrate how they've grown as a character? Can this show how much more they've matured or learned? Can this be a big aha moment that shifts your character's worldview?

Use this prompt for world building.
  Use this prompt for theme.

"What if it's wrong?"

As we get older, we find out that a lot of the things that we learned or were taught are wrong. There are fables, there's mis- education, there's propaganda. There are also just things that we pick up here and there that we take as fact and internalize while they're just false.

What would happen in your current or next scene if your main or perspective character discovered that a long-held belief was wrong?

Is this an opportunity to characterize them? Can your character's re-education of themselves be a major portion of their arc? Will their belief system begin to unravel? Is this a way to show how they were brought up? Can this show the reader where they are in their arc?

Use this prompt for relationships.
Use this prompt for world building.
Use this prompt for theme.

"What I like about you"

No matter how much your intent, humans are judgmental, we see someone interacting in a public space and we are going to pass some form of judgment on them based on how they present themselves and how they act.

What would happen in your current or next scene if your main or perspective character passed judgment on someone else based on that other character's actions or appearance? It doesn't have to be something that they like about them. It can be something that annoys them, maybe just a pet peeve.

Will this help demonstrate to the reader their perspective character's mood at that moment? Can this show the character's maturity? Would the character be less judgmental, or simply judge people differently at different points in the story?

Use this prompt for relationships.
  Use this prompt for world building.

"What are they thinking?"

So as far as I know, none of us are mind readers, and we have navigated through life talking to people whose minds we can't read. But it's also difficult because sometimes we don't know what they're thinking. And we're not sure if they follow what we're saying. And we can't anticipate how they're going to react to certain things.

What would happen in your current or next scene if your main or perspective character focused on not being able to understand what the other character or characters were thinking?

Will that make them speak more carefully? Will it make them over-explain their points? Will it aggravate them? Will it intrigue them?

Use this prompt for relationships.
Use this prompt for world building.

"Weight"

Outside of the gym, health, or engineering, most of us don't think that much about weight. When we go to pick something up, our body adjusts to lift, lift the weight of it, unless it's a surprising weight.

What would happen in your current or next scene if your main or perspective character lifted something of a surprising weight?

Is this a chance to demonstrate the strength of your character? Would the character react differently to this at different points in their arc? Can this show a difference in the character between now and the last time they lifted it?

Use this prompt for world building.

"We don't have time for that"

Now, I don't know about you, when I'm in a time crunch, the closer I get to when something is due, when I'm out of time, the more plans that I had, the more I start abandoning. It doesn't have to be perfect. It doesn't have to have all the bells and whistles. We just have to get it done in time.

What would happen in your current or next scene if your main or perspective character experienced a time crunch and started getting rid of details, plans, or all the extra things that they had been hoping to do?

Can you show the reader how your main character thinks? Can you show how the character prioritized their preparations?

Use this prompt for relationships.
  Use this prompt for plot.

"Try and try again"

"The definition of insanity is trying the same course of action and expecting different results." This is a quote that is vaguely attributed to Albert Einstein even though there are no actual primary sources that say Einstein said this. If anyone has ever practiced any physical sport such as weight training or distance running, you understand that it's simply not true. Truth is, we often reset and try the exact same course of action over and over again and we constantly get different results. In fact, I would say if you're writing a story and your character isn't trying the same course of action multiple times, it might not be believable.

What would happen in your current or next scene if your main or perspective character was trying the same course of action multiple times and they were surprised by the results?

Is this a way to show character growth? Will this challenge the character's fortitude? Can these surprising results change a core belief of your character?

Use this prompt for relationships.

Use this prompt for plot.
Use this prompt for world building.
Use this prompt for theme.

"This will never work"

So, whether it's the big overarching plan or just thinking about what's going to happen in the next scene, characters in our stories have expectations of what's coming next, and usually have a plan of what they're going to do. Oftentimes, they have a best-case scenario in mind, but they also might be pessimistic about what's coming.

What would happen in your current or next scene if your main or perspective character didn't think their plan was going to work?

Is this an opportunity for comedy? Can you reveal something about their character about what they do in the face of adversity? Will you create an interesting internal struggle within themself?

Use this prompt for relationships.

"This is gonna hurt"

A universal idea that unites a lot of humanity is a fear of physical pain. No matter who you are, no matter where you're from, you as an organism are trained, ingrained in a very deep way, to avoid pain in order for your survival. Now, as sentient human beings, we also sometimes have physical pain attached to psychological or emotional situations.

What would happen in your current or next scene if your main or perspective character specifically avoided a physical pain that they were aware of?

Can this create reader empathy for your main character? How does your character deal with their fear of pain throughout the story?

Use this prompt for relationships.
  Use this prompt for plot.

"The worst that could happen"

A big motivator for humans is fear. Fear of something bad that could happen and that will steer our actions or the way that we react to certain things.

What would happen in your current or next scene if your main or perspective character were motivated by fear of something bad that could happen because of their actions? Bonus points if what they fear is something that ultimately happens to them somewhere in the story.

Can this make your character feel more realistic? Is their fear well-founded? Will they stay fear-motivated throughout the story?

Use this prompt for plot.
  Use this prompt for world building.

"The smell of it"

I constantly hear that memory is closer tied to smell than any of the other senses.

What would happen in your current or next scene if your main or perspective character smelled a smell that reminded them of something?

Can this fill out your main character's backstory? Can your character have a strong reaction to this memory? Can the memory relate to what's happening at that point in the story?

Use this prompt for world building.

"The right shoes"

We often don't think about it unless we're wearing the wrong shoes. But the right shoes are super important. They have to fit right. They have to fit the weather. They have to fit the activity that we're doing.

What would happen in your current or next scene if your main or perspective character noticed their shoes in relation to how they move throughout the scene? I am talking about the physical environment.

Can the appropriateness of the shoe say something about your character's fashion sense? Would your reader have a different relationship to their shoe choice at different points in the story? Does your character have an emotional reaction to how the shoes match the ground?

Use this prompt for world building.

"Why it won't work"

This prompt is something that I use throughout the writing process, during drafting, throughout revisions, and once I get notes back from other people. Oftentimes, we're in our own heads about what to do next, especially when a character is planning their next step or in the middle of doing something to achieve their goal. And there are things that they cannot do for certain reasons because it doesn't make sense to the character or because it doesn't make sense for the setting.

What would happen in your current or next scene if your main or perspective character thought through something that wouldn't work, dissecting it either in dialogue or in their head?

Is this a way to make the character's plan seem more logical? Can you give the reader a peek into how the character explicitly thinks? Can the thought process of trial and error stir up big emotions within that character?

Use this prompt for relationships.
 Use this prompt for plot.

Use this prompt for theme.

"That doesn't matter anymore"

S o, at some point in time, things used to matter to your main character that don't matter as much anymore; maybe because of the inciting incident, maybe because of the actions of the plot, maybe because of the relationships that they have forged.

What would happen in your current or next scene if your main or perspective character saw something that reminded them of something that used to matter so much to them...something that just didn't matter that much anymore?

Will this show how much your perspective character has changed since the beginning of the book? Can this remind your reader of everything your character has gone through? Can this make the reader wonder what else will lose priority in the character's mind?

Use this prompt for plot.
  Use this prompt for world building.

"Stillness"

Moments of stillness show up out of the blue, sometimes when you would not expect it, sometimes when you are cultivating it, sometimes when you are cultivating the opposite.

What would happen in your current or next scene if your main or perspective character found a moment of stillness?

Is this an opportunity to underline their mood or emotions? Is your character comfortable in stillness? Where do your character's thoughts go at this moment without any locomotion?

Use this prompt for plot.
  Use this prompt for world building.

"You changed"

Everybody changes, especially characters in a story. And sometimes in real life, when we see how others have changed, it can affect us. We can be proud, ashamed, or even jealous.

So what would happen in your current or next scene if your main or perspective character sensed a change in another character?

Is your main character capable of feeling happy, sad, or otherwise for the other character without centering themselves? Is this a way of tracking your perspective character's arc? Can you show what's changed about your main character through comparison? Is the main character more sensitive to seeing such a change in others?

Use this prompt for relationships.
  Use this prompt for plot.
  Use this prompt for world building.
  Use this prompt for theme.

"Test it out"

As humans, we have running thoughts going all the time. And we might have a thought or a plan that we are afraid to voice or afraid to enact. Maybe we don't think it's going to work, will make us look silly, or make us look incapable.

What would happen in your current or next scene if your main or perspective character voiced a hypothetical that may or may not be exactly their plan just to see what the reaction is?

Can this show your character's thought process in how they present this idea? Can this demonstrate your character's insecurities? Would your character present this hypothetical differently at different parts of the story?

Use this prompt for relationships.
Use this prompt for plot.

"Poker face"

Whether it's an actual secret or even a lie, characters are always withholding things from other characters. Otherwise, it would just be constant nonstop, word vomit.

What would happen in your current or next scene if you focused on your main or perspective character's means of holding back information, like the difference between what they were saying to other characters and what they were thinking?

Since we all do this in real life, can this add a connection between the reader and your character? Can this increase the believability and realism of your character? Can this show your character's inner turmoil, and how your character feels about withholding that information?

Use this prompt for relationships.
    Use this prompt for plot.
    Use this prompt for world building.

"Temperature"

Whether we think about it or not, temperature affects a lot of things, how deep the breath we take is, and how loose our joints and limbs are. The temperature of objects affects how we hold or carry them.

What would happen in your current or next scene if the temperature of the environment or objects affected your main or perspective character's actions?

Does the temperature affect your character's mood? Can sensory elements tie directly to your character's emotions? Does your character become more or less sensitive to temperature throughout their journey?

<u>Use this prompt for plot.</u>
  <u>Use this prompt for world building.</u>

"Moving goalposts"

One of the character arcs that I absolutely love reading is, not only does the character change throughout the story, but they realize that their goal at the beginning of the story is not the same as what they want by the end of the story.

What would happen in your current or next scene if your main or perspective character started to doubt that they actually want their goal?

How does your character internally deal with this doubt? Will they be open about their doubt, or will they continue with the same goal when speaking with other characters?

Use this prompt for theme.

"Smaller or bigger"

Generally speaking as human beings, we have grown. Physically, we used to be smaller, and now we are bigger. From our perspective, sometimes it feels like objects or aspects of our environment have gotten smaller.

What would happen in your current or next scene if your main or perspective character noticed something that used to seem bigger to themselves? Like maybe a piece of clothing, or a landmark?

Is this an opportunity to demonstrate how your main character feels about their past? Can you set up your character arc with a comparison? Did the character have a different worldview back when something used to seem bigger?

Use this prompt for world building.

"Pay attention"

If you're building a complete world for your story, then there are a lot of facets to it. There are a lot of things going on at once, many systems interacting. But despite everything going on, your characters are going to have goals and expectations.

What would happen in your current or next scene if your main or perspective character didn't pay enough attention to what's going on around them, and it caused some sort of failure or extra obstacle?

Can you use this moment to reveal flaws about this character? Will the character learn and grow from this failure? Does the character react emotionally to something they know is their own fault?

Use this prompt for plot.
  Use this prompt for world building.

"The downside"

There are very few plans or ideas that are beneficial to every single party involved. Once you really think about a possible plan and the repercussions, oftentimes you will figure out that there is at least one party or person who is not going to benefit. Someone is going to end up with the short end of the stick.

What would happen in your current or next scene if your main or perspective character realized that someone would not benefit from the ultimate goal? And specifically, someone would be hurt by that goal.

Can this show growth in the character? How empathetic is your character toward those who would be harmed? Does the character learn the potential harm from someone, or do they realize it themselves?

Use this prompt for world building.
Use this prompt for theme.

"News to me"

I n life as well as in stories, we are constantly getting new information. We take that information, react to it, internalize it, then decide what to do and then ultimately, externally react to it. There is a mental and emotional process we go through before immediately reacting to stimuli.

What would happen in your current or next scene if your main or perspective character immediately reacted to stimuli, staying active and foregoing internalization?

Will this focus on action make your characters seem more heroic? Or will it make the reader think them immature or rash? Will this endear them to the reader?

Use this prompt for plot.

"No regrets"

Your character, I imagine, is going to make some decisions as they move through your story. Those decisions will have repercussions.

What would happen in your current or next scene if your main or perspective character wondered whether a decision they made was the wrong one?

Is this a way to pull up the emotional strings of your reader? Is this way you can reinforce what's important to your main character? Can you show the reader what the main characters' expectations are?

"Not the theme"

One of my favorite aspects of a story is the theme, the idea or a question that the author is exploring throughout the story. Very seldom is the theme actually stated within the book. Usually, it is tangential to the main character arc, or even the main character objective. It's the idea that you as the author are exploring; a "What if" or deeper truth that is within the story.

What would happen in your current or next scene if your main or perspective character incorrectly stated the theme? Either said something close to the theme, or just got it completely wrong.

Is this an opportunity to explore a character flaw? Is this a way to trace your character's growth? Can this foreshadow what the character will ultimately learn by the end of the story?

Use this prompt for theme.

"Misunderstanding"

As human beings communicate orally or even through text, there are constant misunderstandings. Our language is just so limited and there's only so much that we can express.

What would happen in your current or next scene if your main or perspective character was misunderstood and actively tried to explain themselves?

What is the reason your character have to explain themselves? Can you tell the reader something about your main character as far as how far they will go without admitting they are wrong? Will the character get frustrated by this process?

Use this prompt for relationships.
  Use this prompt for plot.

"Straight before twist"

In order for a twist in your story to pay off, the reader has to think the story is headed in a clear direction. It has to seem like a hard turn or twist not possible or completely out of the blue, like, not even on the radar of your readers.

What would happen in your current or next scene if you established either such a status quo or such an obvious trajectory of what was going on that the twist seems even more twisted?

Can this make the arc of your main character or even just the arc of the entire plotline incredibly fresh for your reader? Will the main character surprise themselves? Can this help show a more dramatic change in the character from the start to the finish of the book?

Use this prompt for plot.
  Use this prompt for world building.

Relationships

Relationships

Relationships may appear straightforward as a story-telling element, involving how characters interact with each other. However, when crafted skillfully, they become a powerful tool for readers to connect with a story. When readers can recognize similarities between how they relate to people in real life and how a character does, their engagement with the book deepens.

Effective relationships in a story must be realistic, consistent, and dynamic. They should evolve and change over the course of the narrative to keep readers engrossed. Developing relationships with their own arcs adds depth to the storytelling.

"I can't go on"

There are several moments throughout a story in which the main character feels that they have come against an obstacle that is insurmountable: a low point, a dark night of the soul where the main character is farthest from their objective, a losing a moment in the climax. But also, any point in time that your character comes up against an obstacle is an opportunity to show your character doubting themselves, doubting the mission that they're on, doubting the cause that they are championing.

What would happen in your current or next scene if your main or perspective character didn't think that they could defeat the next obstacle?

Will it show their vulnerability, both physically, and in relation to another character? Is this a way to show connection between all of the characters that they have to lean on each other and each other's strengths in order to defeat the next obstacle?

Use this prompt for plot.

"Done differently"

No matter how good of a person you are, there is some level of judgment you levy at others, especially if you witness them performing a task which is within your expertise.

What would happen in your current or next scene if your main or perspective character witnessed someone doing something, and thought about how they would do it differently?

Can this help show their relationship? Is this an opportunity to fill out characterization? Is this a way to keep a character active in an inactive scene?

"A harmless lie"

No matter how much we love the truth or try to be honest with everybody, we can't be 100% honest all the time. We are not just constantly word vomiting our opinions and thoughts, we hold some things back. And oftentimes, we hold back the truth, and we let a lie slip.

Like if someone makes food for you. Sometimes if it's pretty good, but not amazing, you might embellish it a little bit.

"How are you doing today?" 'I'm fine', because we don't want to get into why we're not good.

"How do you like the wine?" 'It's great.' The wine is terrible.

What would happen in your current or next scene if your main or perspective character told a harmless lie?

Can the nature of the lie reveal how the character feels about someone else? Can you show the reader why the relationship drives the character to lie to that other specific character?

Use this prompt for world building.
  Use this prompt for theme.

"Little annoyance"

Fortunately, or unfortunately (depends on how you look at it), we have bodies. We are physical humans as well as mental beings. So, things can happen to us physically, that change our perception of the world around us.

What would happen in your current or next scene if your main or perspective character had a small physical annoyance?

Will it characterize them and show them how quick to temper they are? Can you add dramatic irony by this perspective character dealing with this annoyance, and the other characters not realizing why they're reacting the way they are? Can the way the characters interact add comedy?

Use this prompt for world building.

"They can never know"

I really love the dramatic irony of knowing what's going on inside a character's head versus what's going on externally in the scene. Especially people's opinions of other people, the perspective character's opinion of the characters that they interact with, and how that differs in their head from how they actually act.

What would happen in your current or next scene if your main or perspective character had a very strong opinion about another character that was not revealed through their interaction?

Can you manage to characterize both the perspective character and the other character for the reader? Can you the reader know why the perspective character can't tell the truth about how they feel about the other character? Or maybe you just create comedy by having a perspective character bite their tongue about how they really feel about someone else?

Use this prompt for character arc.
  Use this prompt for world building.

"Unmatched energy"

O ne of the most fun things that I can ever read about is when two characters are interacting and they have completely different energies because of something that one character knows about and that the other one doesn't. Your audience is a part of this. This is a form of dramatic irony.

What would happen in your current or next scene, if your main or perspective character couldn't let the other character know that they knew about something very important?

Could it add comedy? Could it add tension? Will it further develop the relationship between these two characters? Is this a way to let your reader know how much the objective matters to your perspective character as opposed to others?

"Not my speed"

People move at different speeds. People talk with different cadences. Characters move through life at different rhythms.

What would happen in your current or next scene if two characters were moving at two different speeds?

Will it help characterize them by juxtaposing them? Will it create some awkwardness that they will have to work themselves through? Can this just ratchet up tension between characters?

"Keep it together"

S o I imagine in your story, that characters are going to go through some stuff: ideas, emotions, etc. Things are going to hit them to give them a big reaction.

What would happen in your current or next scene if your main or perspective character was trying to keep their reaction to themselves?

Can you show how the character reaction is dependent more upon the character performing the action rather than the action itself? Can you demonstrate how important it is to the character that they not show that other particular character that they care about what occurred? Is this a way of showing how this relationship changes throughout the story?

Use this prompt for character arc.
   Use this prompt for plot.
   Use this prompt for world building.
   Use this prompt for theme.

"Don't say it"

I love dramatic irony, where there is a gap of knowledge between what's going on between the characters and what the characters know and what the reader knows.

What would happen in your current or next scene if your main or perspective character said the opposite of what they were thinking or feeling? I'm talking about the direct opposite. I'm talking about it, "I hate this person..." and then they say, "I love you."

Will that make your character relationships more tense or conflicted? Can you add depth to the relationships in your story? Can this add some levity or much needed comedy in a tense situation?

Use this prompt for character arc.
 Use this prompt for plot.

"Ask around"

F eel free to hit the favorite button and come back to this. There are many ways of figuring things out in the real world. You can study them; you can look things up. Maybe in the world of your story, those things aren't readily available.

Another way of figuring things out is to talk it out with someone else whether or not they are an expert, you ask questions, you use your train of logic.

What would happen in your current or next scene if your main or perspective character worked something out loud? To figure out a big concept that was important to your plot?

Is this a way to develop relationships? Can this help fill out your characters for the reader? Can characters respond to questions in such a way that affects the character asking?

Use this prompt for World Building.

"Don't give it away"

It's always a challenge to keep your character active to make sure that they are moving towards things. They're not becoming passive. They are not just a vehicle for things to happen to.

One obstacle of writing deep perspective fiction is that you can't really describe your character's facial expressions.

What would happen in your current or next scene if your main or perspective character had to hide their reaction? If they had to make sure that their face wasn't betraying what they were thinking?

Can your character wondering if other characters understand what they're thinking add another layer to their relationships? Will the reason your main character doesn't want to give away their reaction further color the relationship?

Use this prompt for plot.

"Difference of opinion"

Something we always have to watch out for, especially if we're new to writing, is differentiating characters, easy ways of doing that are making sure they have different voices, like they use different words. And they describe things differently, making sure that each character has their own goal, and that those goals are different from character to character. But here's another way that we can differentiate them. And that is by opinion, because no two people have the exact same opinion all the way down.

What would happen in your current or next scene if your main or perspective character found out that they had a different opinion of something than another character?

Can this deepen their relationship? Is this an opportunity to create conflict?

Use this prompt for world building.

"Be prepared"

Chances are your characters are preparing or planning for something... Maybe something that is related in some way, shape or form to the climax of your story.

What would happen in your current or next scene if your main or perspective character actively prepared for something coming later, in the midst of something happening now?

Is this an opportunity to show how your characters think? Can you demonstrate relationships by how other characters interact with your character while they're planning? Does each character have a different role in the preparations?

Use this prompt for character arc.
  Use this prompt for plot.
  Use this prompt for theme.

"Don't trust 'em"

Oftentimes in life, we are forced to interact with people that we don't necessarily know and we don't necessarily trust. They can't all be besties.

What would happen in your current or next scene if your main or perspective character had to talk to someone or needed something from someone that they didn't trust? These people don't have to be like enemies or antagonists or anything. They don't have to be nefarious, they could just be like not super responsible, or like, the main character doesn't think much of them.

Is this an opportunity for a colorful supporting character? Can you demonstrate your main character's empathy? Will this create tension?

"Admit it"

We all make all kinds of admissions. Every single day with almost everyone we interact with. Moments of us being vulnerable enough to tell the truth, no matter how important or unimportant, that information is.

What would happen in your current or next scene if your main or perspective character admitted something to another character they were not planning to admit?

Can this deepen the relationship between the characters? Can you use this to surprise your audience? Is what the character admits specific to the other character? Would your character admit something different to another character?

Use this prompt for character arc.

"Absence"

I n our lives, we are constantly feeling the absence of things or people. There are people that we lost along the way. There are people that we have moved away from. They are just situations where other people aren't present and we think about "Oh, that'd be great if this person were here." There are also things, things that we lose, things that we forget, things that we used to associate with certain actions. Sometimes we're going to do those actions without those things there.

What would happen in your current or next scene if your main or perspective character were performing an action and they felt the absence of a person or thing?

Can this make your prose more emotionally rich? Is this an opportunity to make the character more relatable to your reader? Can the relationship to the absent person characterize those present?

Use this prompt for plot.

"I wouldn't say that"

One of the easiest ways to differentiate your characters is by their voice, by their diction: the words that they choose to use, the way they string along sentences. And this can reflect how their brains work differently, how they approach ideas and how they put these ideas together.

What would happen in your current or next scene if two different characters said the same idea with completely different terms?

Is this a way you can characterize your perspective character or main character by juxtaposing them against someone else? Can the characters differ not only in wording, but their positions on an idea? How will the characters interact based on their difference in verbiage?

Use this prompt for world building.
  Use this prompt for theme.

"Forget it"

I don't know about you, but I'm always forgetting stuff. I know I'm old, but like, there's just too much stuff to remember in life.

What would happen in your current or next scene if, while your characters were actively doing something, you reminded the reader of something that that character was forgetting?

Can this forgetfulness characterize this person? How will the other characters react to this forgetfulness? How will the character admit to the other their mistake (or will they admit it at all?)?

Use this prompt for character arc.
  Use this prompt for plot.
  Use this prompt for theme.

"Hierarchy of trust"

People trust in different ways to different degrees. Sometimes you don't trust someone you know to be honest, but you feel like you know them well enough that you know what they're going to do, despite what they say. You trust your knowledge of them. There are people who fill certain roles in your life that you might not trust as much as that role would traditionally dictate a friend or sibling that you know you really can't depend on. Someone that is in the outer edges of your friend circle, that you just trust implicitly.

What would happen in your current or next scene if your main or perspective character said or did something that changed the hierarchy of trust? So that one character that was trusted to some degree is now trusted more or trusted less?

Is this a way to show change in relationships ? Is this a way to let the audience in on your character's values? Can this create tension between characters?

Use this prompt for character arc.
  Use this prompt for plot.

"You don't understand"

Whether we are neurotypical or neurodivergent, it's not always easy to communicate what we are thinking to other people. It's very difficult to get somebody to see through our own perspective, no matter how good we are with words, no matter how well we know the other person, no matter how well we understand the social cues that we share with our audience.

What would happen in your current or next scene if your main or perspective character had a difficult time explaining a thought to another character and had to keep changing tactics?

Can this deepen the connections of some of your character relationships? Can you juxtapose them in how they navigate a difficult conversation? Can you show how they think and speak differently? Can the inability to communicate become a character conflict?

Use this prompt for character arc.
  Use this prompt for plot.
  Use this prompt for world building.

Use this prompt for theme.

112

"Wind down"

Whether it's physical or emotional, there should be some action in your story. But whenever we encounter action in our everyday lives, there is a bit of wind down afterwards, moments of our mind and body trying to return to normal, but sometimes that wind down can get in the way of us wanting to do something else, to immediately start another action. Sometimes it scrambles the brain a little bit so we can't think straight for the next thing.

What would happen in your current or next scene if your main or perspective character's body or mind was winding down, and became an obstacle for what they wanted to do next?

Can the character's inability to shift focus to the next obstacle be a source of conflict? Will your characters wind down from the last occurrence at different paces?

Use this prompt for character arc.
  Use this prompt for plot.
  Use this prompt for world building.

"What if it's wrong?"

As we get older, we find out that a lot of the things that we learned or were taught are wrong. There are fables, there's miseducation, there's propaganda. There are also just things that we pick up here and there that we take as fact and internalize while they're just false.

What would happen in your current or next scene if your main or perspective character discovered that a long-held belief was wrong?

Can this cause conflict between characters? Will characters have different relationships with these beliefs? Can one character direct another in their discovering of the truth?

Use this prompt for character arc.
   Use this prompt for world building.
   Use this prompt for theme.

"What I like about you"

No matter how much your intent, humans are judgmental; we see someone interacting in a public space and we are going to pass some form of judgment on them based on how they present themselves and how they act.

What if your main or perspective character passed judgment on someone else based on that other character's actions or appearance? It doesn't have to be something that they like about them. It can be something that annoys them, maybe just a pet peeve.

Is the judgment based on the character's pre-existing relationship? Will this snap judgment conflict with how the characters wind up relating? Can this be a fun way of creating conflict or mistrust at the beginning of a relationship?

Use this prompt for character arc.
  Use this prompt for world building.

"What are they thinking?"

So as far as I know, none of us are mind readers, and we have navigated through life talking to people whose minds we can't read. But it's also difficult because sometimes we don't know what they're thinking. And we're not sure if they follow what we're saying. And we can't anticipate how they're going to react to certain things.

What would happen in your current or next scene if your main or perspective character focused on not being able to understand what the other character or characters were thinking?

Can your character pigeon-hole the other character is a certain type of person unique to your world? Will the conflict of not understanding one another be a major sticking point in their relationship? Will the misunderstanding create a conflict in an otherwise affable relationship?

Use this prompt for character arc.
  Use this prompt for world building.

"We don't have time for that"

Now, I don't know about you, when I'm in a time crunch, the closer I get to when something is due, when I'm out of time, the more plans that I had, the more I start abandoning. It doesn't have to be perfect. It doesn't have to have all the bells and whistles. We just have to get it done in time.

What would happen in your current or next scene if your main or perspective character was experiencing a time crunch and got rid of details or plans or all the extra things that they had been hoping to do?

Can this abandoning cause conflict between characters? Can this juxtapose two different characters in how they deal with a time crunch?

Use this prompt for character arc.
  Use this prompt for plot.

"Try and try again"

"The definition of insanity is trying the same course of action and expecting different results." This is a quote that is vaguely attributed to Albert Einstein even though there are no actual primary sources that say Einstein said this. If anyone has ever practiced any physical sport such as weight training or distance running, you understand that it's simply not true. Truth is, we often reset and try the exact same course of action over and over again and we constantly get different results. In fact, I would say if you're writing a story and your character isn't trying the same course of action multiple times, it might not be believable.

What would happen in your current or next scene if your main or perspective character was trying the same course of action multiple times and they were surprised by the results?

Can other characters have opinions on the repeated attempts? Will other characters be surprised or unsurprised by the results? Will the results make other characters feel differently moving forward about this character?

Use this prompt for character arc.
  Use this prompt for plot.
  Use this prompt for world building.
  Use this prompt for theme.

"Downplay"

Within a story, things are always being revealed to characters, especially your perspective character (hopefully).

What would happen in your current or next scene if your main or perspective character tried to downplay their reaction to a new piece of information?

Can you show the juxtaposition between what is going on in the character's interior versus what's going on in the exterior? Is this an opportunity for comedy?Can you reveal how that character feels about other characters by what they're thinking as they're talking to them?

"This will never work"

S o, whether it's the big overarching plan or just thinking about what's going to happen in the next scene, characters in our stories have expectations of what's coming next, and usually have a plan of what they're going to do. Oftentimes, they have a best-case scenario in mind, but they also might be pessimistic about what's coming.

What would happen in your current or next scene if your main or perspective character didn't think their plan was going to work?

What do other characters think of their pessimism? Does the pessimism distinguish this character from others? Can this lead to larger reactions of how the scene plays out?

Use this prompt for character arc.

"This is gonna hurt"

A universal idea that unites a lot of humanity is a fear of physical pain. No matter who you are, no matter where you're from, you as an organism are trained, ingrained in a very deep way, to avoid pain in order for your survival. Now, as sentient human beings, we also sometimes have physical pain attached to psychological or emotional situations.

What would happen in your current or next scene if your main or perspective character specifically avoided a physical pain that they were aware of?

Can you compare how two characters deal with their fear of pain? Is a fear of pain a possible way for your characters to connect?

Use this prompt for character arc.
  Use this prompt for plot.

"Why it won't work"

This prompt is something that I use throughout the writing process, during drafting, throughout revisions and once I get notes back from other people. Oftentimes, we're in our own heads about what to do next, especially when a character is planning their next step, or in the middle of doing something to achieve their goal. And there are things that they cannot do for certain reasons, because it doesn't make sense to the character or because it doesn't make sense for the setting.

What would happen in your current or next scene if your main or perspective character thought through something that wouldn't work, dissecting it either in dialogue or in their head.

Can out-loud thinking be a point of conflict between characters? Can this distinguish how your characters think and approach problems differently? Can the thought process affect how the character think of each other?

Use this prompt for character arc.
  Use this prompt for plot.

Use this prompt for theme.

"What's unsaid"

There's a subtext to everything that goes on in life, there is a context that isn't explicitly stated. And I imagine there's a subtext in a lot of what's going on in your story.

What would happen in your current or next scene if your main or perspective character focused on the subtext, not about what was being said between characters, but what wasn't being said? Maybe there was some eye contact? Some facial expressions? Things to let the reader know that there was a lot of stuff going on that they weren't saying out loud.

Will this add wrinkles in relationships between your characters? Can you paint questions in your readers' minds about relationships without explicitly stating things? Will this make your characters feel more real?

Use this prompt for plot.

"You changed"

Everybody changes, especially characters in a story. And sometimes in real life, when we see how others have changed, it can affect us. We can be proud, ashamed, or even jealous.

So what would happen in your current or next scene if your main or perspective character sensed a change in another character?

Can this foreshadow the other characters' arc? Can this create tension in their relationship? Can this shift their power dynamic?

Use this prompt for character arc.
  Use this prompt for plot.
  Use this prompt for world building.
  Use this prompt for theme.

"Test it out"

As humans we have running thoughts going all the time. And we might have a thought or a plan that we are afraid to voice or afraid to enact. Maybe we don't think it's going to work, will make us look silly, or make us look incapable.

What would happen in your current or next scene if your main or perspective character voiced a hypothetical that may or may not be exactly their plan just to see what the reaction is?

Is this a way to characterize all the other characters listening? Can this solidify their relationship to your readers? Will this conversation demonstrate their relationships naturally?

Use this prompt for character arc.
  Use this prompt for plot.

"Poker face"

Whether it's an actual secret or even a lie, characters are always withholding things from other characters. Otherwise, it would just be constant nonstop, word vomit.

What would happen in your current or next scene if you focused on your perspective character's means of holding back information, like the difference between what they were saying to other characters and what they were thinking?

Can you reveal how your character feels about lying to others? Can this cause a rift in a character relationship? What if one character knows the reasoning behind withholding this information and it actually draws them closer?

Use this prompt for character arc.
    Use this prompt for plot.
    Use this prompt for world building.

"Misunderstanding"

As human beings communicate orally or even through text, there are constant misunderstandings. Our language is just so limited and there's only so much that we can express.

What would happen in your current or next scene if your main or perspective character was misunderstood and actively tried to explain themselves?

Can this ramp up conflict between characters? How will different characters react to this misunderstanding? How patient is your character explaining to the others?

Use this prompt for character arc.
  Use this prompt for plot.

"Reveal"

Sometimes I find out that people that I've worked with, known for years, or have become close with are gay. Because gay people exist. Queer people, gay, lesbian, trans, ace, aro people just exist. Their existence doesn't have to be the point of a story or move the plot along. Nor do they need to come out or specify the nuance of their gender.

What would happen in your current or next scene if a character let another character know that they were gay?

Can this make your cast of characters more interesting by not making them completely homogeneous as far as sexual identity goes? Can this add nuance to relationships by finding out about possible attraction (or the impossibility of attraction) later in a story?

Use this prompt for world building.
  Use this prompt for theme.

Plot

Not to oversimplify, but the plot of the story is the collection of external events and actions. Enjoyable plots require active characters, conflict, tension (which is the presence of interesting questions in the reader's mind), and a continuous series of consequences — an unbroken chain of cause-and-effect.

One challenge in crafting a compelling plot lies in maintaining all of these elements consistently. No scene or chapter can lack conflict, deflate tension, or break the chain of consequences. While main characters must appear active, there are some tricks a writer can employ to allow secondary or tertiary characters to carry the actions.

If a writer can keep all of these aspects of plot going, they will achieve a feeling of constant escalation that can make a book difficult to put down.

"Match the pace"

Sometimes, a more difficult facet of writing to catch onto, especially when you're a beginner, is pace. Pacing is how the action unfolds, but also the rate at which your prose can be read and move that action forward. For example, if the pacing is slow when a character is in their own head, observing a scene, thinking ideas, and remembering moments in their life. Whereas if a character is dealing with present, immediate action, or even action sequences within flashbacks, that is a quicker pace.

What would happen in your current or next scene if you matched the pace of your prose to the pace of what was happening in the story?

Can you show how the character is conflicted, or bogged down in their own thoughts or feelings because things are going slowly? Can you use that slow pace to string tension and describe the character's fear or focus? Can you show how quickly an action sequence feels to a character by rushing through the description? Can you barely touch on feelings that you can unpack later on through dialogue?

"The why"

Your main character is probably doing stuff in your story, right? Things to do, probably doing it for a reason, a reason that's good to them.

What if, in your next scene and maybe all of your scenes, you figured out a way to sprinkle in an escalation of the importance of this 'why'?

I'm not talking about how the outside forces interact with your character and make that character's reasoning for what they're doing, for their quest, for their adventure, for the plot to get increasingly more complex or higher stakes. I am talking about your main character, thinking about the 'why' that's motivating them. And as they think about it, they take apart that concept and realize that it's more and more important than they first realized.

Will this make your main character more likable to the reader now that they understand what motivates them better? Will this get your reader much more invested in what's going on? Will this drive your readers to keep going to get to the next chapter to keep turning the page?

<u>Use this prompt for theme.</u>

"Don't say it"

I am absolutely obsessed with this idea and I love it when it shows up in books: the best-case scenario, that every character walks into every scene with an idea in mind about how this interaction is going to go. And no matter what, it never goes absolutely perfectly, and they have to improvise it.

What would happen in your current or next scene if your main or perspective character was planning on saying something to another character, but because of what happens in the duration of a scene, they decided against it?

Are they now worried that information is going to come out before they can say it? Is that idea now consuming them and driving them? Are they withholding information to be kind? Are they withholding information to be cruel? Does this withholding of information somehow escalate the circumstances?

Use this prompt for character arc.
  Use this prompt for relationships.

135

"I can't go on"

There are several moments throughout a story in which the main character feels that they have come against an obstacle that is unsurmountable: a low point, a dark night of the soul where the main character is farthest from their objective, a losing a moment in the climax. But also, any point in time that your character comes up against an obstacle is an opportunity to show your character doubting themselves, doubting the mission that they're on, doubting the cause that they are championing.

What would happen in your current or next scene if your main or perspective character didn't think that they could defeat the next obstacle?

Will it add an even bigger payoff when they do? Is this an opportunity to prepare the reader to experience failure with the character?

<u>Use this prompt for relationships.</u>

"What does it feel like?"

I heard this concept a while ago and I cannot get it out of my mind. So, I'm going to tell you about it, and it's your problem now... If you look at anything, your tongue can determine what it would feel like. Your tongue can know the texture based on what you see. Now we don't have to involve the tongue in there. If you look at something, your mind can predict what texture it is.

What would happen in your current or next scene if no matter what's going on, your main or perspective character imagined the texture of something in their physical surroundings?

Will it make the scene feel more realistic? Will it distract your character from what's going on in the scene to give it a bigger impact later on? Can the focus on texture move the plot forward?

Use this prompt for world building.

"I've got a bad feeling about this"

Going into every scene, characters have something in mind about what's going to happen just like we do in real life. We intend to talk to our boss about a raise, we intend to talk to our partner about our day, we intend to talk to our dog about getting a treat.

What would happen in your current or next scene if your main or perspective character had a bad feeling about what was going to happen next?

Will the outcome surprise them? Can you foreshadow something that's going to happen later in the book? Can you color the mood of this point in the story with their pessimism?

Use this prompt for character arc.

"The ground"

Most people, as they move through their life, their day, or any space, have a surface underneath them. Something they walk on, something they roll on, something that they move along, whether it's floor, a walkway, or the ground.

What would happen in your current or next scene if you added a detail about the ground that in some way, shape or form affected the story?

Can a character noticing this detail be a form of foreshadowing? Can the ground somehow become an obstacle in that scene? Can the terrain indicate the character's physical proximity to a goal? Can you create dramatic irony by making an obstacle that the reader will know about that the character doesn't know about it yet?

Use this prompt for character arc.
  Use this prompt for world building.

"Surprise"

N ow, I don't know about you, but in my everyday life, I'm constantly surprised by things; mostly because I have a four- year-old daughter, but also because the world is an amazing place and things are constantly happening, and I don't know it all.

What would happen in your current or next scene if your main or perspective character was surprised by something?

Will it make them more realistic to your reader? Will you be able to foreshadow what the character is expecting versus what is going to happen? Is there a way to pay into a big payoff that's going to happen later?

Use this prompt for character arc.
.Use this prompt for world building.

"I can't remember"

U nless it's intrinsic in the plot or for a specific payoff or point, stories don't often use lapses of memory, like the fact that a character can't remember a face that they can't place. But in reality, it happens all the time (maybe that's just me, I am old).

What would happen in your current or next scene if your main or perspective character had a difficult time remembering something?

Is this an opportunity to keep your character internally active when they might otherwise be passive? Can the dramatic irony of the reader waiting for the character to remember string along tension? Can the character incorrectly remember something that complicates the scene?

Use this prompt for world building.

"Pay in"

So, every single well-crafted story has payoffs. Around the end, there are things that come back which have been alluded to. These payoffs achieve emotional impact because the reader has an expectation, then they happen or they don't happen. Either way, readers are finally given some sort of closure. Now, the only way for these things to emotionally resonate is if the readers have an opinion of the payoff happening (they want these things to happen, or not to happen or afraid they're going to happen or afraid they're not gonna happen). That means just starting in motion this idea that something might or might not happen is not enough. You have to continually allude to it; you have to pay in so it pays off in the end.

How can you pay into an idea that has nothing to do with your current or next scene, but has everything to do with a payoff that's happening later?

Maybe you can make the reader fear an upcoming plot point. Can you remind the reader what importance this thing has to your plot? Can you create dramatic irony by making an action mean a lot more to the reader than the character?

Use this prompt for character arc.

"Keep it together"

S o I imagine in your story, that characters are going to go through some stuff: ideas, emotions, etc. Things are going to hit them to give them a big reaction.

What would happen in your current or next scene if your main or perspective character was trying to keep their reaction to themselves?

Is it important to the plot that the character not react? Can the character keep active by internally struggling with not reacting aloud or visibly?

Use this prompt for character arc.
   Use this prompt for relationships.
   Use this prompt for world building.
   Use this prompt for theme.

"You can't see it from here"

The world around us affects how we perceive the world around us. If I am looking through a window outside in that window is dirty, then that affects how I see the world outside. Or, looking at someone but the light is in my eye, that affects how I look at that person. My hair going across my glasses affects how I see things. Is there a way in your story that the setting, the world around, the perspective character or the main character can affect how they perceive things? Maybe in a literal sense, maybe not in a literal sense, maybe by way of their socio-economic status, employment status, relationship with their house.

What would happen in your current or next scene if your main or perspective character realized and focused on how much the world around them is affecting how they perceive things?

Can the obstruction change throughout the story as a way of tracking how close the character is to that goal? Can different obstructions demonstrate different moments in the plot? Can the obstruction become an obstacle that must be surpassed for the character to continue?

<u>Use this prompt for character arc.</u>
   <u>Use this prompt for world building.</u>
   <u>Use this prompt for theme.</u>

"Angry words"

Mood is the emotional atmosphere of a scene. In movies, they'll use camera tricks and lighting, literally, where they placed the camera and how it looks at the character and sometimes other effects like fog, to establish mood.

But in writing, we have our words, we have the prose, a great way to establish mood is your diction.

What would happen in your current or next scene if you chose your words to reinforce the atmosphere of the scene or the mood of the main or perspective character?

Can you increase the gravity of a scene important to your plot? Can you draw your reader's attention to some detail as a form of foreshadowing? Is this an opportunity to describe the same object in two different moods to escalate tension as you move toward a climax?

Use this prompt for character arc.
  Use this prompt for theme.

"Diverging paths"

I n life, and probably in your story, people (characters) have choices. Maybe this is a choice of two things between two paths to take. Maybe it's more than that.

What would happen in your current or next scene if your main or perspective character had to decide between two things and thought about what the future would be like with either choice?

Is this an opportunity to demonstrate your character's imagination? Can you foreshadow what's going to happen later in the story? Is this a way to manipulate your readers' expectations for what happens next?

Use this prompt for character arc.

"Figure it out"

Someone smarter than me once said that every book is a mystery to the reader. After all, the reader is figuring out every aspect of the story as they go along, unlocking a mystery of what it's about and what the characters are doing and why they're doing it. But the truth is, every scene that your character walks into is a mystery. And they are figuring things out. They're figuring out what's going on, and they're gleaning new information.

What would happen in your current or next scene if you focused on how the main or perspective character got new information and figured things out?

Can the mystery of the scene add tension? Can the character's investigation within the scene drive an otherwise inactive scene? Can the information the character discovers drive some of the action moving forward.

Use this prompt for character arc.

"Exhilaration"

After doing something incredibly physically demanding, some- thing that seemed impossible, or even something as simple as solving a riddle, you get this little hit of serotonin. You get some adrenaline. You get exhilarated.

What would happen in your current or next scene if your main or perspective character is exhilarated, but they had to power through that to work on the next thing, to do the next thing, to solve the next problem?

Can this indicate to the reader how big of a moment something was for them? Will they show how many difficult things they have to deal with one after another? Is this an opportunity to show the reader the character's priorities?

Use this prompt for character arc.

"Don't give it away"

I t's always a challenge to keep your character active to make sure that they are moving towards things. They're not becoming passive. They are not just a vehicle for things to happen to.

One obstacle of writing deep perspective fiction is that you can't really describe your character's facial expressions.

What would happen in your current or next scene if your main or perspective character had to hide their reaction? If they had to make sure that their face wasn't betraying what they were thinking?

Is this a way to keep your character active in a passive scene? Will your characters attempt to create tension? Can exterior forces further the plot while your main character is attempting to stay stone-faced?

Use this prompt for relationships.

"Don't listen"

One big thing that being a dad has taught me is that it is difficult for kids to think about what they're doing while they're doing it because they just are so excited about doing it. And that makes sense because that's not just exclusive to kids. Oftentimes as adults, while we're doing something that is important to us we forget everything that we're supposed to remember and we just do it.

What would happen in your current or next scene if your main or perspective character did something the wrong way because they were not thinking about the steps that they needed to take while they did it?

They realize that they are doing things the wrong way and that they are not taking the correct steps and they still cannot correct it while they are doing the thing.

Will this garner empathy from your readers? Will this tighten up the tension in the scene? Is this a try/fail cycle that makes the payoff at the end bigger?

Use this prompt for character arc.

"Discomfort"

In most societies we are encumbered with things that we wear, as well as hair, sometimes glasses, sometimes contacts, all of these things have the potential to give us physical discomfort.

What would happen in your current or next scene if your main or perspective character actively worked against a physical discomfort as they moved through the scene?

Can this add to the tension you're already building? Is this a way to keep a character active in an inactive scene?

Use this prompt for character arc.
   Use this prompt for world building.

"Be prepared"

C hances are your characters are preparing or planning for something... Maybe something that is related in some way, shape or form to the climax of your story.

What would happen in your current or next scene if your main or perspective character actively prepared for something coming later, in the midst of something happening now?

Is this a way to set up plot points for your reader? Can you create expectations you can later subvert? Is this a way to foreshadow a twist?

Use this prompt for character arc.
  Use this prompt for relationships.
  Use this prompt for theme.

"Absence"

In our lives, we are constantly feeling the absence of things or people. There are people that we lost along the way. There are people that we have moved away from. They are just situations where other people aren't present and we think about "Oh, that'd be great if this person were here." There are also things, things that we lose, things that we forget, things that we used to associate with certain actions. Sometimes we're going to do those actions without those things there.

What would happen in your current or next scene if your main or perspective character were performing an action and they felt the absence of a person or thing?

Can you use this to foreshadow? Can the absence of a certain character hinder what the characters are attempting?

Use this prompt for relationships.

"Irksome"

There's a lot of things that might get under our skin. There are things that we might dislike, there are preferences, pet peeves, but sometimes, there are things that we don't like, and we can't explain why we don't like them.

What would happen in your current or next scene if your main or perspective character ran into something that annoyed them, but they couldn't put their finger on it.

Can this ratchet up tension? Can the annoyance make whatever the goal of the scene more difficult? Can the annoyance become an important plot point later in the story?

Use this prompt for character arc.

"How it used to be"

As I get older and slowly turn into my parents, one thing that I notice that I do all the time is talk about how things are different. As I drive around, I'm like, "Oh, that used to be a grocery store," or "that building is going up fast" or "I remember when this used to be farmland," and all of that really boring old people stuff.

What would happen in your current or next scene if your main or perspective character focused on a change that they noticed in their setting or characters around them?

Could that be a physical description that represents the changes in the plot of the world of your book? Could changes in the world indicate the dangers of the overarching conflict of the story?

Use this prompt for character arc.
  Use this prompt for world building.

"Mirrored failure"

A big obstacle when writing a book is making sure that your main character is staying active. Passive characters can be unrelatable and cause the reader to dislike them or lose interest in your story. You can really bog your whole book down. Some traps that can cause passive characters are flashbacks, observing, and long descriptions. If they're not directly related to an active scene or an action, such traps can slow reader momentum or even bore them into putting the story down.

What would happen in your current or next scene if your main or perspective character remembered a time they acted and failed as it related to an action in the present scene?

Can this show how daunting their task or mission is? Is this a way to track the actions of the character over time? Can this show the important of the character goal without explicitly spelling it out?

Use this prompt for character arc.
  Use this prompt for worldbuilding.

Use this prompt for theme.

"Mental checklist"

Now, I don't know about you guys, but I go through mental checklists all the time, and not just when I'm doing something big and important. But also like, every time I leave a place, every time I go to drive someplace, I'm going through a lit of what I need- wallet, phone, keys, and probably a snack just in case.

As an author, I do a lot of in-person events. And for those in-person events, I'm often doing a mental checklist and often realizing that I forgot something.

What would happen in your current or next scene if your main or perspective character was preparing to do something (it doesn't have to be a big thing), and as they're doing a mental checklist, they realize they've forgotten something? Then, they have to determine how important that thing is.

Will this string tension along? Can this show the importance or lack of importance of what they're about to do? Can the lack of that item complicate the next action they must do?

<u>Use this prompt for character arc.</u>

"Little by little"

U nless you're writing a pretty short story, your characters are probably going to have to go through a lot of steps toward their goal. Whether or not they achieve that goal, there's going to be many steps along the way. Oftentimes, when we're focused on the goals, these tiny steps that we take seem too small for our patience, seem like we're not making progress, seem like the goal is that much further away.

What would happen in your current or next scene if the main or perspective character started getting frustrated with the very small amount of progress that they were making towards an overarching goal?

Can you reinforce how important a goal is to them? Can their frustration become a self-imposed obstacle in a smaller scene goal? Can this check-in on their progress be a way of mapping out the journey of the plot to the reader?

Use this prompt for character arc.
  Use this prompt for world building.

"Forget it"

I don't know about you, but I'm always forgetting stuff. I know I'm old, but like, there's just too much stuff to remember in life.

What would happen in your current or next scene if while your characters were actively doing something, you reminded the reader of something that that character is forgetting?

Can this produce an obstacle the characters must overcome? Can the character's forgetfulness endanger other characters? Can you use this dramatic irony to increase the tension within the scene?

Use this prompt for character arc.
  Use this prompt for relationships.
  Use this prompt for theme.

"Hierarchy of trust"

People trust in different ways to different degrees. Sometimes you don't trust someone you know to be honest, but you feel like you know them well enough that you know what they're going to do, despite what they say. You trust your knowledge of them. There are people who fill certain roles in your life that you might not trust as much as that role would traditionally dictate a friend or sibling that you know you really can't depend on. Someone that is in the outer edges of your friend circle, that you just trust implicitly.

What would happen in your current or next scene if your main or perspective character said or did something that changed the hierarchy of trust? So that one character that was trusted to some degree is now trusted more or trusted less?

Can the change in relationships alter the trajectory of your character(s)? Will different decisions be made according to whom is where in this new hierarchy? Can the hierarchy establish obstacles for your characters?

Use this prompt for character arc.

Use this prompt for relationships.

"Helpless"

One thing that I like to focus on as a person is controlling my controllables and understanding what is out of my control. And that's a pretty simple thing to say, but not a simple thing to do. There are things that are always out of our control, that can frustrate us, that can get in our way, that can ruin our plans. These things can sometimes seem in our control when they're not, or vice versa.

What would happen in your current or next scene if your main or perspective character focused on what is out of their control?

*Be careful with this prompt because you don't want your main character to be passive.

Is this a way to show how big and impactful the action of the plot is? Can their frustration become a self-imposed obstacle?

Use this prompt for character arc.
  Use this prompt for world building.

"From a distance"

I f your story has a deep perspective, either first person or close third person, then you cannot step out of that character to look at anything. But, your character can guess or think about what things look like from afar.

What would happen in your current or next scene if your main or perspective character took a distant look at the situation that they were in? This could mean literal or figurative. Just a look at what the actions they are involved in look like from afar.

Is this a quiet tableau moment before action happens? Is this an opportunity to show the before and after of a major plot point? Can the way the characters look foreshadow what will happen to them?

Use this prompt for character arc.
  Use this prompt for world building.

"You don't understand"

Whether we are neurotypical or neurodivergent, it's not always easy to communicate what we are thinking to other people. It's very difficult to get somebody to see through our own perspective, no matter how good we are with words, no matter how well we know the other person, no matter how well we understand the social cues that we share with our audience.

What would happen in your current or next scene if your main or perspective character was having a difficult time explaining a thought to another character and had to keep changing tactics?

Can explaining one issue in several ways solidify parts of your plot for your reader? Can the character's frustration or inability to communicate become an obstacle for the characters to overcome? Can this conflict escalate the tension in the scene?

Use this prompt for character arc.
  Use this prompt for relationships.

<u>Use this prompt for world building.</u>
<u>Use this prompt for theme.</u>

"You can't do that"

Satisfying character arcs are the ones that finish with the main character doing something that seemed absolutely impossible for them to do. And I'm not talking about a superhuman feat. I'm talking about something that internally, you wouldn't think that the character was capable of because of trauma or emotions. They come to admit that they needed help, or for them to trust someone else.

What would happen in your current or next scene if your main or perspective character alluded to not being able to do the one thing that you know that they're going to have to do in the climax? If you just reinforced that there's no way that this character is going to be able to do that?

Is this an opportunity to foreshadow? Can the character experience some try/fail cycles as a way to add conflict along the story's rising action? Can you add a failed attempt within the scene in order to keep the character active?

Use this prompt for character arc.
  Use this prompt for theme.

171

"Wind down"

Whether it's physical or emotional, there should be some action in your story. But whenever we encounter action in our everyday lives, there is a bit of wind down afterwards, moments of our mind and body trying to return to normal, but sometimes that wind down can get in the way of us wanting to do something else, to immediately start another action. Sometimes it scrambles the brain a little bit so we can't think straight for the next thing.

What would happen in your current or next scene if your main or perspective character's body or mind was winding down, and became an obstacle for what they wanted to do next?

Is this an opportunity to show how defeated they are in a try fail cycle? Can this underline the physical toll of the action they're doing? Can the inability to wind down quickly become a source of conflict?

Use this prompt for character arc.
  Use this prompt for relationships.
  Use this prompt for world building.

172

"We don't have time for that"

ow, I don't know about you, when I'm in a time crunch, the closer I get to when something is due, when I'm out of time, the more plans that I had, the more I start abandoning. It doesn't have to be perfect. It doesn't have to have all the bells and whistles. We just have to get it done in time.

What would happen in your current or next scene if your main or perspective character experienced a time crunch and started getting rid of details or plans or all the extra things that they had been hoping to do?

Can this demonstrate how serious the stakes are for the time crunch? Can this make the time crunched goal feel more impossible? Can the abandoned plans make obstacles later?

Use this prompt for character arc.
  Use this prompt for relationships.

"Try and try again"

"The definition of insanity is trying the same course of action and expecting different results." This is a quote that is vaguely attributed to Albert Einstein even though there are no actual primary sources that say Einstein said this. If anyone has ever practiced any physical sport such as weight training or distance running, you understand that it's simply not true. Truth is, we often reset and try the exact same course of action over and over again and we constantly get different results. In fact, I would say if you're writing a story and your character isn't trying the same course of action multiple times, it might not be believable.

What would happen in your current or next scene if your main or perspective character was trying the same course of action multiple times and they were surprised by the results?

Can this add to your try/fail cycle? Can this attempt be a metaphor for a larger conflict in the story? Can the surprising result disrupt the story's rising action?

Use this prompt for character arc.

Use this prompt for relationships.
Use this prompt for world building.
Use this prompt for theme.

"This is gonna hurt"

A universal idea that unites a lot of humanity is a fear of physical pain. No matter who you are, no matter where you're from, you as an organism are trained, ingrained in a very deep way, to avoid pain in order for your survival. Now, as sentient human beings, we also sometimes have physical pain attached to psychological or emotional situations.

What would happen in your current or next scene if your main or perspective character specifically avoided a physical pain that they were aware of?

Can this make your story feel more realistic? Is this an opportunity to ratchet up the tension? Will this make bigger obstacles feel less possible to the reader?

Use this prompt for character arc.
  Use this prompt for relationships.

176

"The worst that could happen"

A big motivator for humans is fear. Fear of something bad that could happen and that will steer our actions or the way that we react to certain things.

What would happen in your current or next scene if your main or perspective character were motivated by fear of something bad that could happen because of their actions? Bonus points if what they fear is something that ultimately happens to them somewhere in the story.

Could this be foreshadowing? Can this fear be a source of conflict or obstacles throughout the story? Can the fear come back to confront the character in a way that escalates a later conflict?

Use this prompt for character arc.
   Use this prompt for world building.

"The inevitable"

I've heard a lot of people say that a really good ending or climax to a story should be surprising, but when you think about it, it was inevitable. And I think that that can go for a climax of everything in the story (chapter, scene, act, arc, etc) because after all, whatever the structure of your whole book is, or your whole story, those structures should be able to be seen in miniature for every scene, as every chapter sightings and rising action, climax, falling action.

What would happen in your current or next scene if you fore-shadowed throughout what the inevitable climax or conclusion to that scene was without explicitly stating it?

Will this lead to a bigger emotional payoff for your reader? Will this make the scene feel more complete? Is this a way to build reader momentum and investment so they keep going?

"Why it won't work"

This prompt is something that I use throughout the writing process, during drafting, throughout revisions and once I get notes back from other people. Oftentimes, we're in our own heads about what to do next, especially when a character is planning their next step, or in the middle of doing something to achieve their goal. And there are things that they cannot do for certain reasons, because it doesn't make sense to the character or because it doesn't make sense for the setting.

What would happen in your current or next scene if your main or perspective character thought through something that wouldn't work, dissecting it either in dialogue or in their head.

Is this a way to keep a character active during a planning process? Can you show your reader that you are actively trying to think of everything to get the characters out of the situation or towards their goal?

Use this prompt for character arc.
  Use this prompt for relationships.

Use this prompt for theme.

"What's unsaid"

There's a subtext to everything that goes on in life, there is a context that isn't explicitly stated. And I imagine there's a subtext in a lot of what's going on in your story.

What would happen in your current or next scene if your main or perspective character focused on the subtext, not about what was being said between characters, but what was not being said? Maybe there was some eye contact? Some facial expressions? Things to let the reader know that there's a lot of stuff going on that they aren't saying out loud.

Will this string along the tension? Can you make the reader wonder about events that affect the story?

Use this prompt for relationships.

"That doesn't matter anymore"

So, at some point in time, things used to matter to your main character that don't matter as much anymore; maybe because of the inciting incident, maybe because of the actions of the plot, maybe because of the relationships that they have forged.

What would happen in your current or next scene if your main or perspective character saw something that reminded them of something that used to matter so much to them...something that just didn't matter that much anymore?

Will this demonstrate the importance of the plot and the actions of your main character? Can this remind your reader of everything your character has gone through? Will this just be a little detail that adds to the realism in your book as we all grow up in things that matter to us change?

Use this prompt for character arc.
Use this prompt for world building.

"Stillness"

Moments of stillness show up out of the blue, sometimes when you would not expect it, sometimes when you are cultivating it, sometimes when you are cultivating the opposite.

What would happen in your current or next scene if your main or perspective character found a moment of stillness?

Is this a breath in the middle of action? Is this stillness a way of drawing out the tension of what is to come? How can you keep your character active for the reader within a moment of stillness?

Use this prompt for character arc.
  Use this prompt for world building.

"You changed"

Everybody changes, especially characters in a story. And sometimes in real life, when we see how others have changed, it can affect us. We can be proud, ashamed, or even jealous.

So what would happen in your current or next scene if your main or perspective character sensed a change in another character?

Is this an opportunity to create tension? Can the role another character plays in the plot change? Is this an opportunity to foreshadow conflict or redemption later in the story?

Use this prompt for character arc.
 Use this prompt for relationships.
 Use this prompt for world building.
 Use this prompt for theme.

"Test it out"

As humans we have running thoughts going all the time. And we might have a thought or a plan that we are afraid to voice or afraid to enact. Maybe we don't think it's going to work, will make us look silly, or make us look incapable.

What would happen in your current or next scene if your main or perspective character voiced a hypothetical that may or may not be exactly their plan just to see what the reaction is?

Can the discussion set reader's expectations and understanding of an upcoming series of actions in the plot? Can the reactions foreshadow what could go right or wrong? Is this an opportunity to mirror the overall plot in miniature with a smaller goal being discussed?

Use this prompt for character arc.
  Use this prompt for relationships.

"Poker face"

Whether it's an actual secret or even a lie, characters are always withholding things from other characters. Otherwise, it would just be constant nonstop, word vomit.

What would happen in your current or next scene if you focused on your main or perspective character's means of holding back information, like the difference between what they were saying to other characters and what they were thinking?

Can this keep your character active in an otherwise inactive scene? Can this withholding of information be a plot point later in the story?

Use this prompt for character arc.
  Use this prompt for relationships.
  Use this prompt for world building.

"Temperature"

Whether we think about it or not, temperature affects a lot of things, how deep the breath we take is, how loose our joints and limbs are. The temperature of objects affects how we hold or carry them.

What would happen in your current or next scene if the temperature of the environment or objects affected your main or perspective character's actions?

Do these details begin to explain your character's actions? Can your character''s physical reaction to temperature cause tension, conflict, or a wrinkle in rising action?

Use this prompt for character arc.
  Use this prompt for world building.

"Pay attention"

If you're building a complete world for your story, then there are a lot of facets to it. There are a lot of things going on at once, many systems interacting. But despite everything going on, your characters are going to have goals and expectations.

What would happen in your current or next scene if your main or perspective character didn't pay enough attention to what's going on around them, and it caused some sort of failure or extra obstacle?

Can this be a try/fail cycle that makes your character more endearing? Can this small obstacle or failure indicate an overarching conflict in your plot? Can a self-imposed obstacle like this add agency to an otherwise passive scene?

Use this prompt for character arc.
  Use this prompt for world building.

"News to me"

I n life as well as in stories, we are constantly getting new information. We take that information, react to it, internalize it, then decide what to do and then ultimately, externally react to it. There is a mental and emotional process we go through before immediately reacting to stimuli.

What would happen in your current or next scene if your main or perspective character immediately reacted to stimuli, staying active and foregoing internalization?

Can this increase the pace of your story? Will your character have serious moments later on fully comprehending the implications of what happened? Will the character act so quickly that they make an error?

Use this prompt for character arc.

"Misunderstanding"

A s human beings communicate orally or even through text, there are constant misunderstandings. Our language is just so limited and there's only so much that we can express.

What would happen in your current or next scene if your main or perspective character was misunderstood and actively tried to explain themselves?

Is this an opportunity for comedy? Can you explain a difficult plot point through reiterating? Will the misunderstanding escalate and become an important conflict?

Use this prompt for character arc.
  Use this prompt for relationships.

"Straight before twist"

I n order for a twist in your story to pay off, the reader has to think the story is headed in a clear direction. It has to seem like a hard turn or twist not possible or completely out of the blue, like, not even on the radar of your readers.

What would happen in your current or next scene if you established either such a status quo or such an obvious trajectory of what was going on that the twist seems even more twisted?

Can you establish such a clear direction that the twist feels bigger? Is this a way to allow your reader into a false sense of security? Will this create an unexpected yet inevitable climax to the story?

<u>Use this prompt for character arc.</u>
  <u>Use this prompt for world building.</u>

World Building

World Building is setting. But let's be honest, it sounds cooler to work on world building.

Every setting in a story requires both a physical presence, encompassing how it looks, feels, sounds, and even smells, as well as a contextual humanity. This includes aspects like its history, economic systems, social interactions, politics (which essentially involves the exchange of power among people), and even its approach to sciences. Magic systems and technology also play a significant role in world building. However, many books are set in a world similar to our own, and explaining this familiar reality is still a form of world building.

One challenge to keep in mind is that the characters in the story typically have no knowledge of a world beyond their own. When drawing comparisons between our real-life experiences and the world of the story, such thoughts and dialogues often read as unnatural or overly expository.

"When it all changed."

A lmost all of us are different than we were when we were younger. And for many of us, there is a specific point in time in which our worldview or our ideas about the nature of humanity changed.

What would happen in your current or next scene if your main or perspective character juxtaposed what they would have thought of a situation before and after their worldview changed?

Will this fill out your setting and make the world you build full of stakes? Can this illustrate commonly held beliefs in your world?

Use this prompt for character arc.

"A harmless lie"

No matter how much we love the truth or try to be honest with everybody, we can't be 100% honest all the time. We are not just constantly word vomiting our opinions and thoughts, we hold some things back. And oftentimes, we hold back the truth, and we let a lie slip.

Like if someone makes food for you. Sometimes if it's pretty good, but not amazing, you might embellish it a little bit.

"How are you doing today?" 'I'm fine', because we don't want to get into why we're not good.

"How do you like the wine?" 'It's great.' The wine is terrible.

What would happen in your current or next scene if your main or perspective character told a harmless lie?

Can you let the reader know more about your character's moral compass and how they feel about these tiny lies? Will it make your character appear more realistic to the reader? Can you reveal something about the society of the world in your book and how people interact with each other and use these small lies?

Use this prompt for relationships.
  Use this prompt for theme.

"What does it feel like?"

I heard this concept a while ago and I cannot get it out of my mind. So, I'm going to tell you about it, and it's your problem now... If you look at anything, your tongue can determine what it would feel like. Your tongue can know the texture based on what you see. Now we don't have to involve the tongue in there. If you look at something, your mind can predict what texture it is.

What would happen in your current or next scene if no matter what was going on, your main or perspective character imagined the texture of something in their physical surroundings?

Will it make the scene feel more realistic? Will it enrich your world with detail? Will it ground your character and reader?

Use this prompt for plot.

"This is completely normal"

There is like a 99% chance that the world of your story is different from the world of your reader, even if it's realistic fiction or even a memoir, your everyday life is going to be different from your reader's life and you have to establish that. Specifically, you need to establish what the normal is before whatever changes and makes the story interesting starts happening.

Because remember, for a little farm boy who had to herd his sheep away from the giant fire-breathing dragon, herding sheep away from giant fire-breathing dragons is probably a mundane task. It's probably annoying and maybe a little bit boring.

What would happen in your current or next scene if your main or perspective character engaged in an activity boring to them, but amazing to your reader?

Can this establish your character's socioeconomic status? Can this specify something normal to your character's vocation, but perhaps abnormal to most characters in the world?

"Little annoyance"

Fortunately, or unfortunately (depends on how you look at it), we have bodies. We are physical humans as well as mental beings. So, things can happen to us physically, that change our perception of the world around us.

What would happen if in your current or next scene your main or perspective character had a small physical annoyance?

Can it be a physical annoyance that's unique to your setting and do some world building for you? Can this add comedy?

Use this prompt for relationships.

"They can never know"

I really love the dramatic irony of knowing what's going on inside a character's head versus what's going on externally in the scene. People's opinions of other people, the perspective character's opinion of the characters that they interact with, and how that differs in their head from how they actually act.

What would happen in your current or next scene if your main or perspective character had a very strong opinion about another character that was not revealed through their interaction?

Can you do some world building and let the reader know about the hierarchy or the social norms that don't allow the perspective character to tell the truth about how they feel about the other character? Or maybe you just create comedy by having a perspective character bite their tongue about how they really feel?

Use this prompt for character arc.
  Use this prompt for relationships.

"Surprise"

N ow, I don't know about you, but in my everyday life, I'm constantly surprised by things; mostly because I have a four-year-old daughter, but also because the world is an amazing place and things are constantly happening, and I don't know it all.

What would happen in your current or next scene if your main or perspective character was surprised by something?

Is this an opportunity to show the reader what is "normal" in the setting of your story? Can you establish any special aspect or powers of your character by showing what is surprising?

Use this prompt for character arc.
  Use this prompt for plot.

199

"The ground"

Most people, as they move through their life, their day, or any space, have a surface underneath them. Something they walk on, something they roll on, something that they move along, whether it's floor, a walkway, or the ground.

What would happen in your current or next scene if you added a detail about the ground that in some way, shape or form affected the story?

Is this a detail that can add to the richness of your world? Do people in this world have a relationship with the ground that people in real life don't? Is the flooring unique to your world?

Use this prompt for character arc.
  Use this prompt for world building.

"Keep it together"

S o I imagine in your story, that characters are going to
go through some stuff: ideas, emotions,etc. Things are
going to hit them to give them a big reaction.

What would happen in your current or next scene if your main
or perspective character was trying to keep their reaction to
themselves?

Can you add depth to why the thing matters so much to that
character in your world? Can you demonstrate societal norms
by focusing on what reaction isn't socially acceptable? Is this
an opportunity to depict the social hierarchy by your character
not reacting to the actions of a character of a higher or lower
social class?

Use this prompt for character arc.
  Use this prompt for relationships.
  Use this prompt for plot.
  Use this prompt for theme.

"You can't see it from here"

The world around us affects how we perceive the world around us. If I am looking through a window outside in that window is dirty, then that affects how I see the world outside. Or, looking at someone but the light is in my eye, that affects how I look at that person. My hair going across my glasses affects how I see things. Is there a way in your story that the setting, the world around, the perspective character or the main character can affect how they perceive things? Maybe in a literal sense, maybe not in a literal sense, maybe by way of their socio-economic status, employment status, relationship with their house.

What would happen in your current or next scene if your main or perspective character realized and focused on how much the world around them is affecting how they perceive things?

Will it make the world feel more realistic to the reader? Can the obstruction be unique to your world? By describing this obstruction, can you describe something in the world without an info-dump?

Use this prompt for character arc.
  Use this prompt for plot.
  Use this prompt for theme.

"Ask around"

Feel free to hit the favorite button and come back to this. Now there are many ways of figuring things out in the real world. You can study them; you can look things up. Maybe in the world of your story, those things aren't readily available.

Another way of figuring things out is to talk it out with someone else whether or not they are an expert, you ask questions, you use your train of logic.

What would happen in your current or next scene if your main or perspective character worked something out loud? To figure out a big concept that was important to your plot?

Is this a way of actively world building without just throwing information? Can the way a character responds relay wide held beliefs in the world of your story? Can the character being asked avoid answering about certain subjects as a way of showing the reader what is forbidden, taboo, or powerful?

Use this prompt for relationships.

"Easier said than done"

Oftentimes, we can talk a big game about an action that is harder than we expected. Or sometimes we bluster on purpose to show off.

What would happen in your current or next scene if your main or perspective character had to complete some action based on a declaration they had made earlier? It doesn't have to be as big as independence or bankruptcy, it can be simply saying, "I am going to do this." We are now this and now their actions associated with it that maybe they did or did not foresee.

Is this a way to demonstrate how the character has to act in order to fulfill those declarations? Can you show an action specific to the world of your story that is difficult? Is this an opportunity to show off societal norms in how the character made the declaration in the first place?

Use this prompt for character arc.
  Use this prompt for theme.

"Distraction"

T he world is constantly moving around us, things keep going, no matter how focused we are, no matter how singularly important our goal is.

What would happen in your current or next scene if your main or perspective character had a difficult time looking through the distractions and focusing on their objective or goal?

Can you add realism and texture to the world with these distractions? Can distractions unique to your world make the reader think the character goal isn't as important as originally thought?

Use this prompt for character arc.

"Difference of opinion"

Something we always have to watch out for, especially if we're new to writing, is differentiating characters, easy ways of doing that are making sure they have different voices, like they use different words. And they describe things differently, making sure that each character has their own goal, and that those goals are different from character to character. But here's another way that we can differentiate them. And that is by opinion, because no two people have the exact same opinion all the way down.

What would happen in your current or next scene if your main or perspective character found out that they had a different opinion of something than another character?

Can you relay information about the world to your reader by having characters discuss differences in opinion? Can you show each character's socioeconomic status in that difference? Can you demonstrate differences of belief systems?

Use this prompt for relationships.

"Detail in motion"

In emotional situations, we can find ourselves focusing on a small physical detail. And actually oftentimes, people like professional athletes they train themselves to focus on one specific detail and the movement or difference in that detail will determine what they then do. Think batters watching a pitcher's arm, or a hockey player watching the puck.

What would happen in your next scene if your perspective character or main character focused on a physical detail that changes throughout the action.

Can you add to the details of the world by describing this detail and showing how it changes? Will this make the world feel more real to your reader? Is this a way to focus your action sequences.

"Discomfort"

I n most societies we are encumbered with things that we wear, as well as hair, sometimes glasses, sometimes contacts, all of these things have the potential to give us physical discomfort.

What would happen in your current or next scene if your main or perspective character actively worked against a physical discomfort as they moved through the scene?

Is this an opportunity to world build? Can that uncomfortable piece of clothing or whatever it is, be intrinsic to that character's culture? Can you show how the peoples within your story's world deal with that discomfort?

Use this prompt for character arc.
  Use this prompt for plot.

"Future is history"

S ometimes it's difficult to see, but everything happening around us is happening in a time period that will one day be history. Seeing the context of where this time period will fit and what it will be looked back upon as and what it will lead to is often difficult.

What would happen in your current or next scene if your main or perspective character thought about how their current time period will be looked upon in the future? And this doesn't just apply to history-changing events, or giant plots that affect a lot of people. They can just look at the time period and think how will people look back on this?

Can you explain the history of your world in context? Can you show how history is viewed and studied? Will it signify the importance of the plot to the world?

Use this prompt for character arc.

"I wouldn't say that"

O ne of the easiest ways to differentiate your characters is by their voice, by their diction: the words that they choose to use, the way they string along sentences. And this can reflect how their brains work differently, how they approach ideas and how they put these ideas together.

What would happen in your current or next scene if two different characters said the same idea with completely different terms?

Is this an opportunity to fill out how different characters of the world feel about similar ideas? Can this show different belief systems within your world? Can this show difference in class, education, or socialization?

Use this prompt for relationships.
  Use this prompt for theme.

"How it used to be"

As I get older and slowly turn into my parents, one thing that I notice that I do all the time is talk about how things are different. As I drive around, I'm like, "Oh, that used to be a grocery store," or "that building is going up fast" or "I remember when this used to be farmland," and all of that really boring old people stuff.

So what would happen in your current or next scene if your main or perspective character focused on a change that they noticed in their setting or characters around them?

Could that make the setting feel more realistic? Can you sneak in some history without an info-dump? Is this a way to clearly describe the character's surroundings organically?

Use this prompt for character arc.
  Use this prompt for plot.

"Mirrored failure"

A big obstacle when writing a book is making sure that your main character is staying active. Passive characters can be unrelatable and cause the reader to dislike them or lose interest in your story. You can really bog your whole book down. Some traps that can cause passive characters are flashbacks, observing, and long descriptions. If they're not directly related to an active scene or an action, such traps can slow reader momentum or even bore them into putting the story down.

What would happen in your current or next scene if your main or perspective character remembered a time they acted and failed as it relates to an action in the present scene?

Is this an opportunity to show an action (such as a rite of passage or ceremony) unique to your world? Can you walk the reader through an event that is normal to the characters of the world organically? Is this a way to show how the world has changed over time?

Use this prompt for character arc.

<u>**Use this prompt for plot.**</u>
<u>**Use this prompt for theme.**</u>

"Little by little"

Unless you're writing a pretty short story, your characters are probably going to have to go through a lot of steps toward their goal. Whether or not they achieve that goal, there's going to be many steps along the way. Oftentimes, when we're focused on the goals, these tiny steps that we take seem too small for our patience, seem like we're not making progress, seem like the goal is that much further away.

What would happen in your current or next scene if the main or perspective character started getting frustrated with the very small amount of progress that they were making towards an overarching goal?

Can you express distance from the goal as physical distance in world building? Can you express a metric of improvement (example: getting better at magic) as a way of revealing the workings of your world to the reader? Can the way the character expressed frustration be unique to the world of the story?

<u>Use this prompt for character arc.</u>
<u>Use this prompt for plot.</u>

"I can't remember"

Unless it's intrinsic in the plot or for a specific payoff or point, stories don't often use lapses of memory, like the fact that a character can't remember a face that they can't place. But in reality, it happens all the time (maybe that's just me, I am old).

What would happen in your next scene if your perspective character or main character had a difficult time remembering something?

Can you fill out the reality of your world as your character searches their memory? Can something in the world of your story be the cause for confusion or forgetfulness? Can the character go through a series of incorrect answers that not only escalate tension, but also give your reader more glimpses into the world of the story?

Use this prompt for plot.

"Helpless"

O ne thing that I like to focus on as a person is controlling my controllables and understanding what is out of my control. And that's a pretty simple thing to say, but not a simple thing to do. There are things that are always out of our control, that can frustrate us, that can get in our way, that can ruin our plans. These things can sometimes seem in our control when they're not, or vice versa.

What would happen in your current or next scene if your main or perspective character focused on what is out of their control?

*Be careful with this prompt because you don't want your main character to be passive.

Can you solidify your world building by showing the reader what is out of the control of your worlds' inhabitants? Can their frustrations organically give the reader information about the world?

Use this prompt for character arc.
  Use this prompt for plot.

"From a distance"

I f your story has a deep perspective, either first person or close third person, then you cannot step out of that character to look at anything. But, your character can guess or think about what things look like from afar.

What would happen in your current or next scene if your main or perspective character took a distant look at the situation that they were in? This could mean literal or figurative. Just a look at what the actions they are involved in look like from afar.

Can this help paint the picture of the setting for your reader? Can you describe a bigger scale look at the setting organically?

Use this prompt for character arc.
  Use this prompt for plot.

"In relation to"

When describing scenery, or anything physical to be honest, it's easy to just describe it at face value, or even go a step forward and imbue the description with the emotion of the character.

What would happen in your current or next scene, if you described anything physical in terms of how it helps the character reach their next and most immediate goal?

Is this a way to describe physical surroundings in a new light? Will this make something like a description feel more active? Will this give the immediate setting of each scene more important context?

Use this prompt for character arc.

"Holiday"

U nless the world of your story is vastly different from our own, then there are anniversaries, birthdays, and holidays that take place. And as you may or may not know, almost every single day has some sort of assigned significance to it, whether it commemorates a person, an action or an idea.

What would happen in your current or next scene if it took place during a holiday specific to the world of your book?

Can this holiday have a different meaning internally for your main character or perspective character than it does for everyone else? Can you reveal your character by showing their attitude about this holiday? Is this an opportunity to tell something about the world with what the day commemorates? Will the way your character feels about the holiday reveal beliefs in the world?

Use this prompt for character arc.

"You don't understand"

Whether we are neurotypical or neurodivergent, it's not always easy to communicate what we are thinking to other people. It's very difficult to get somebody to see through our own perspective, no matter how good we are with words, no matter how well we know the other person, no matter how well we understand the social cues that we share with our audience.

What would happen in your current or next scene if your main or perspective character had a difficult time explaining a thought to another character and had to keep changing tactics?

Can you explain a setting, socioeconomic issue, or belief in depth by the character reiterating themselves? Can the inability of the characters to communicate be based in the character's different roles in the story's society?

Use this prompt for character arc.
  Use this prompt for relationships.
  Use this prompt for plot.
  Use this prompt for world building.

"Wind down"

Whether it's physical or emotional, there should be some action in your story. But whenever we encounter action in our everyday lives, there is a bit of wind down afterwards, moments of our mind and body trying to return to normal, but sometimes that wind down can get in the way of us wanting to do something else, to immediately start another action. Sometimes it scrambles the brain a little bit so we can't think straight for the next thing.

What would happen in your current or next scene if your main or perspective character's body or mind was winding down and became an obstacle for what they wanted to do next?

Can the difficulty to wind down relate to your setting? Are there ways of recuperating that are unique to your world? Would characters from different social groups recover differently?

Use this prompt for character arc.
  Use this prompt for relationships.
  Use this prompt for plot.

"What's changed?"

Oftentimes as we get older, we learn more context about the world around us and understand things more. We can see the same piece of information, memory, or object and understand it better. We have learned, we have grown, we just get the context more than we did the first time that we encountered it.

What would happen in your current or next scene if your main or perspective character revisited a memory, an object, or an idea with a new context and realized that there is an added meaning or a different meaning entirely?

Is this an opportunity to foreshadow? Can a character epiphany move the plot along? Can this realization foreshadow something to come? Can a reconfiguring of knowledge keep a character active in an otherwise passive scene?

Use this prompt for character arc.
  Use this prompt for theme.

"What if it's wrong?"

As we get older, we find out that a lot of the things that we learned or were taught are wrong. There are fables, there's miseducation, there's propaganda. There are also just things that we pick up here and there that we take as fact and internalize while they're just false.

What would happen in your current or next scene if your main or perspective character discovered that a long-held belief was wrong?

Can this show widely-held beliefs in the world? Is this a way of examining the world's history without info-dumping? Is this particular society divided by people who still believe this lie and those who know the truth?

Use this prompt for character arc.
  Use this prompt for relationships.
  Use this prompt for theme.

"What I like about you"

No matter how much your intent, humans are judgmental, we see someone interacting in a public space and we are going to pass some form of judgment on them based on how they present themselves and how they act.

What if your perspective character or main character passed judgment on someone else based on that other character's actions or appearance? It doesn't have to be something that they like about them. It can be something that annoys them, maybe just a pet peeve.

Will this illustrate the main character's worldview? Is this an opportunity to show how people act in the world of your story? Can you discuss trends and styles in your world in an organic way?

Use this prompt for character arc.
  Use this prompt for relationship.

"What are they thinking?"

So as far as I know, none of us are mind readers, and we have navigated through life talking to people whose minds we can't read. But it's also difficult because sometimes we don't know what they're thinking. And we're not sure if they follow what we're saying. And we can't anticipate how they're going to react to certain things.

What would happen in your current or next scene if your main or perspective character focused on not being able to understand what the other character or characters were thinking?

Can your character wonder if the other character is a certain type of person unique to your world? Is this type of miscommunication common in your world?

Use this prompt for character arc.
  Use this prompt for relationships.

"Weight"

O utside of the gym, health, or engineering, most of us don't think that much about weight. When we go to pick something up, our body adjusts to lift, lift the weight of it, unless it's a surprising weight.

What would happen in your current or next scene if your main or perspective character lifted something of a surprising weight?

Is this a world building opportunity to show a unit of measurement? Can this detail make the world of your story feel more realistic? Can the fact that he weight is surprising add to the lore of your world?

Use this prompt for character arc.

"Try and try again"

"The definition of insanity is trying the same course of action and expecting different results." This is a quote that is vaguely attributed to Albert Einstein even though there are no actual primary sources that say Einstein said this. If anyone has ever practiced any physical sport such as weight training or distance running, you understand that it's simply not true. Truth is, we often reset and try the exact same course of action over and over again and we constantly get different results. In fact, I would say if you're writing a story and your character isn't trying the same course of action multiple times, it might not be believable.

What would happen in your current or next scene if your main or perspective character character is trying the same course of action multiple times and they are surprised by the results?

What do people of the world of your book think about these continued attempts? Is the description of multiple attempts an opportunity to organically explain a detail of your world more clearly?

Use this prompt for character arc.
  Use this prompt for relationships.
  Use this prompt for plot.
  Use this prompt for theme.

"The worst that could happen"

A big motivator for humans is fear. Fear of something bad that could happen and that will steer our actions or the way that we react to certain things.

What would happen in your current or next scene if your main or perspective character were motivated by fear of something bad that could happen because of their actions? Bonus points if what they fear is something that ultimately happens to them somewhere in the story.

Are the worst-case scenarios filling out your world? Can your world have unique stakes? What's the worst thing that could happen in that world of your story?

Use this prompt for character arc.
  Use this prompt for plot.

"The smell of it"

I constantly hear that memory is closer tied to smell than any of the other senses.

What would happen in your current or next scene if your main or perspective character smelled a smell that reminded them of something?

Will this make the setting feel more realistic to the reader? Can the source of the scent be unique to the world? Will adding more senses make the world more immersive?

Use this prompt for character arc.

"The right shoes"

We often don't think about it unless we're wearing the wrong shoes. But the right shoes are super important. They have to fit right. They have to fit the weather. They have to fit the activity that we're doing.

What would happen in your current or next scene if your main or perspective character noticed their shoes in relation to how they move throughout the scene? I am talking about the physical environment.

Can this help the world build? Can the newness or type of shoe say something about your world's socio-economic norms? Can you describe the terrain organically by relating them to footwear?

Use this prompt for character arc.

"That doesn't matter anymore"

S o, at some point in time, things used to matter to your main character that don't matter as much anymore; maybe because of the inciting incident, maybe because of the actions of the plot, maybe because of the relationships that they have forged.

What would happen in your current or next scene if your main or perspective character saw something that reminded them of something that used to matter so much to them...something that just didn't matter that much anymore?

Will this show what matters to people in your world? Is something that matter more to younger people than older? Can you explain an aspect of your world by explaining the character's change in opinion?

Use this prompt for character arc.
  Use this prompt for plot.

"Stillness"

Moments of stillness show up out of the blue, sometimes when you would not expect it, sometimes when you are cultivating it, sometimes when you are cultivating the opposite.

What would happen in your current or next scene if your main or perspective character found a moment of stillness?

Can you use this opportunity to describe the surroundings? Does the world of your story have any beliefs around stillness, tranquility, or moments without productivity that can be explored?

Use this prompt for character arc.
  Use this prompt for plot.

"You changed"

Everybody changes, especially characters in a story. And sometimes in real life, when we see how others have changed, it can affect us. We can be proud, ashamed, or even jealous.

What would happen in your current or next scene if your main or perspective character sensed a change in another character?

Can the change indicate something unique to your story's world? Can the change in character be a common transition people go through in this world? Is this change going to affect how this other character moves in the world going forward?

Use this prompt for character arc.
   Use this prompt for relationships.
   Use this prompt for plot.
   Use this prompt for theme.

"Poker face"

Whether it's an actual secret or even a lie, characters are always withholding things from other characters. Otherwise, it would just be constant nonstop, word vomit.

What would happen in your current or next scene if you focused on your main or perspective character's means of holding back information, like the difference between what they are saying to other characters and what they are thinking?

Can this withholding of information be unique to the world of your story? Can you characterize a group of people in this world by showing what one character won't reveal? Is there an understanding among any characters that a certain type of person wouldn't be open about a specific topic?

Use this prompt for character arc.
  Use this prompt for relationships.
  Use this prompt for plot.

"Temperature"

Whether we think about it or not, temperature affects a lot of things, how deep the breath we take is, how loose our joints and limbs are. The temperature of objects affects how we hold or carry them.

What would happen in your current or next scene if the temperature of the environment or objects affected your main or perspective character's actions?

Is this a way to make the setting feel more real? Can you use this opportunity to describe an object or place unique to your world? Is there a world building aspect, like a ritual, trend, or environmental state that influences temperature?

Use this prompt for character arc.
  Use this prompt for world building.

"Smaller or bigger"

Generally speaking as human beings, we have grown. Physically, we used to be smaller, and now we are bigger. From our perspective, sometimes it feels like objects or aspects of our environment have gotten smaller.

What would happen in your current or next scene if your perspective character or your main character noticed something that used to seem bigger to themselves? Like maybe a piece of clothing, or a landmark?

Will the background make your character feel more realistic? Is this an opportunity to talk about the world organically? Can you go into detail about objects, how they look, and how they're made to fill out the world?

Use this prompt for character arc.

"Pay attention"

If you're building a complete world for your story, then there are a lot of facets to it. There are a lot of things going on at once, many systems interacting. But despite everything going on, your characters are going to have goals and expectations.

What would happen in your current or next scene if your main or perspective character didn't pay enough attention to what was going on around them, and it caused some sort of failure or extra obstacle?

Is this an opportunity to reveal more about the world? Can systems within this society constantly obstruct people of this world, but your character notices this for the first time? Are there physical dangers in the setting the character hadn't realized?

Use this prompt for character arc.
  Use this prompt for plot.

"The downside"

There are very few plans or ideas that are beneficial to every single party involved. Once you really think about a possible plan and the repercussions, oftentimes you will figure out that there is at least one party or person who is not going to benefit. Someone is going to end up with the short end of the stick.

What would happen in your current or next scene if your main or perspective character realized that someone would not benefit from the ultimate goal? And specifically, someone would be hurt by that goal.

Will this make the world feel more realistic? Can you reveal something about how the systems of the world works through who would be harmed? Is this an opportunity to show economic and class systems?

Use this prompt for character arc.
 Use this prompt for theme.

"Straight before twist"

I n order for a twist in your story to pay off, the reader has to think the story is headed in a clear direction. It has to seem like a hard turn or twist not possible or completely out of the blue, like, not even on the radar of your readers.

What would happen in your current or next scene, if you established either such a status quo or such an obvious trajectory of what was going on that the twist seems even more twisted?

Can this cementing the norms and expectations fill out some of your world building? Can the expectations of the characters mirror that of the reader? Can you stretch what the reader thought was possible in this world?

<u>Use this prompt for character arc.</u>
  <u>Use the prompt for world building.</u>

"Reveal"

Sometimes I find out that people that I've worked with, known for years, or have become close with are gay. Because gay people exist. Queer people, gay, lesbian, trans, ace, aro people just exist. Their existence doesn't hve to be the point of a story or move the plot along. Nor do they need to come out or specify the nuance of their gender.

What would happen in your current or next scene if a character let another character know that they're gay?

Is this a way of making your world feel more realistic? Are gender and sexual identity treated differently in the world of your story?

Use this prompt for relationships.
   Use this prompt for theme.

Theme

A theme is the central thesis or question that an author explores throughout a story. It's often not explicitly stated within the text but can sometimes be found in the opening hook of a well-written blurb.

One common storytelling device is the 'statement of theme,' which typically occurs before the inciting incident. This device is especially prevalent in chapter books and middle-grade literature, where a mentor character may advise the main character with something like, 'You can't just go through life...' followed by an action or belief that embodies the story's theme. In these cases, the character's development (arc) is almost always directly linked to the overarching theme.

Themes can encompass broad ideas with cultural, sociological, and political implications, but they can also revolve around intimate concepts, such as how a single person's actions can lead to profound change or form unexpected relationships.

"Micro theme, macro theme"

Theme is the big idea of the story that is almost never explicitly stated. It could be the moral. It could be a philosophical question. It can be a political issue. It's a topic from the real world that your book references, but not directly addressed in the world of your book, if that makes sense.

What would happen in your current or next scene if you gave an example of your theme in miniature? What about an example of the theme taken to the extreme?

For example, if you wrote a book with the theme about common-sense gun reform, then what would happen if you gave a character a nuclear weapon? What if there was a young child who had a spitball?

Is this a way to allow your reader to connect the dots without explicitly stating something? Can you lead the reader to think of real-life implications by talking about overblown or under-whelming examples of the theme in practice? Can you use this to sew the theme into your world building? Is this an opportunity for your story's characterization to intrinsically connect to your theme?

"The why"

Your main character is probably doing stuff in your story, right? Things to do, probably doing it for a reason, a reason that's good to them.

What if in your current or next scene and maybe all of your scenes, you figured out a way to sprinkle in an escalation of the importance of this 'why'?

I'm not talking about how the outside forces interact with your character and make that character's reasoning for what they're doing, for their quest, for their adventure, for the plot to get increasingly more complex or higher stakes. I am talking about your main character, thinking about the 'why' that's motivating them. And as they think about it, they take apart that concept and realize that it's more and more important than they first realized.

Use this prompt for plot.

"Distill"

Whether you mean to or not, all stories written have a bigger idea whether it's a theme, or whether the plot is actually a universal struggle. These are things that readers can connect to and can draw a line from the real world into their book, and readers will make these connections whether you mean to write them into your story or not. It makes more sense for you to do it with intention and control how you approach that with intent, rather than not think about it and leave things up to reader interpretation and perchance let the reader completely get what your perspective is, incorrect.

What would happen in your current or next scene if your main or perspective character saw something that was the theme or the universal struggle in macrocosm. Whether it's a quick exchange in dialogue or literally seeing the way two animals play with each other or looking at the dynamic of ants on the ground?

Is this a way to clarify your theme? Can your character's goals and motivations underline your reasons for writing this story?

Will this get your reader much more invested in your theme?
Will this drive your readers to keep going to get to the next
chapter to keep turning the page?

"What is this change?"

All the time in the world around us, things are constantly changing, but especially in stories. Otherwise, there would be no story, and all conditions would be completely stagnant. Things are changing in your story.

What would happen in your current or next scene if your main or perspective character didn't understand a change that directly related to your theme?

Can you reveal more about the theme by showing how they would react to this change that they are uncertain of? Can you foreshadow something awesome to reveal later on? Can you create dramatic irony by letting the reader know what's happening but the perspective character doesn't get it?

Use this prompt for character arc.

"Big feelings"

I think one of the most difficult aspects of "show, don't tell" is when it comes to feelings and reactions and emotions. Not blatantly using the word sad, happy, surprised, but unpacking what that feels like to experience those.

What if in your current or next scene, you took the biggest emotion experienced by your perspective character and unpacked it without using that word?

Can you describe the feeling in a more universal way so that the reader can feel it at the same time? Can you ground the feeling in the physical attribute of the character? Can the words you choose to encapsulate the feeling evoke the theme?

Use this prompt for character arc.

"A harmless lie"

No matter how much we love the truth or try to be honest with everybody, we can't be 100% honest all the time. We are not just constantly word vomiting our opinions and thoughts, we hold some things back. And oftentimes, we hold back the truth, and we let a lie slip.

Like if someone makes food for you. Sometimes if it's pretty good, but not amazing, you might embellish it a little bit.

"How are you doing today?" 'I'm fine', because we don't want to get into why we're not good.

"How do you like the wine?" 'It's great.' The wine is terrible.

What would happen in your current or next scene if your main character or perspective character told a harmless lie?

Can you let the reader know more about your character's moral compass and how they feel about these tiny lies? Can you use this lie as a fixed point on a scale of morality to help drive your theme?

<u>Use this prompt for relationships.</u>
  <u>Use this prompt for world building.</u>

"Keep it together"

S o I imagine in your story, that characters are going to go through some stuff: ideas, emotions,etc. Things are going to hit them to give them a big reaction.

What would happen in your current or next scene if your main or perspective character was trying to keep their reaction to themselves?

Can you add depth to why the thing matters so much to that character by getting their inner dialogue going? Can you reinforce themes by focusing on how this character is going to keep it together and not reveal what matters so much to them?

Use this prompt for character arc.
   Use this prompt for relationships.
   Use this prompt for plot.
   Use this prompt for world building.

"You can't see it from here"

The world around us affects how we perceive the world around us. If I am looking through a window outside in that window is dirty, then that affects how I see the world outside. Or, looking at someone but the light is in my eye, that affects how I look at that person. My hair going across my glasses affects how I see things. Is there a way in your story that the setting, the world around, the perspective character or the main character can affect how they perceive things? Maybe in a literal sense, maybe not in a literal sense, maybe by way of their socio-economic status, employment status, relationship with their house.

What would happen in your current or next scene if your main or perspective character realized and focused on how much the world around them is affecting how they perceive things?

Will it reinforce your theme? Can whatever affects your fictional character's perception be a metaphor for your theme? Can that perception obstacle be a thing that exists in the real world?

<u>Use this prompt for character arc.</u>
   <u>Use this prompt for plot.</u>
   <u>Use this prompt for world building.</u>

"Angry words"

Mood is the emotional atmosphere of a scene. In movies, they'll use camera tricks and lighting, literally, where they placed the camera and how it looks at the character and sometimes other effects like fog, to establish mood.

But in writing, we have our words, we have the prose, a great way to establish mood is your diction.

What would happen in your current or next scene if you chose your words to reinforce the atmosphere of the scene or the mood of the main or perspective character?

Can you increase the gravity of a scene important to your theme? Is this an opportunity to describe the same object in two different moods to reveal something about your theme?

Use this prompt for character arc.
  Use this prompt for plot.

"Diverging paths"

I n life, and probably in your story, people, characters have choices. Maybe this is a choice of two things between two paths to take. Maybe it's more than that.

What would happen in your current or next scene if your main or perspective character had to decide between two things and thought about what the future would be like with either choice?

Is this an opportunity to demonstrate two opposing aspects of the question that is your theme? Can walking through hypothetical situations encourage your reader to think about hypothetical situations in their own life?

Use this prompt for character arc.
  Use this prompt for plot.

"Easier said than done"

Oftentimes, we can talk a big game about an action that is harder than we expected. Or sometimes we bluster on purpose to show off.

What would happen in your current or next scene if your main or perspective character had to complete some action based on a declaration they had made earlier? It doesn't have to be as big as independence or bankruptcy, it can be simply saying, "I am going to do this." Once they get to that point, now their actions associated with it that maybe they did or did not foresee.

Is this an opportunity for one of those this-was-harder-than-I-thought kind of moments to underline your theme? Can you indirectly state the real-life difficulties and implications of the theme?

Use this prompt for character arc.
  Use this prompt for theme.

"Be prepared"

Chances are your characters are preparing or planning for something... Maybe something that is related in some way, shape or form to the climax of your story.

What would happen in your current or next scene if your main or perspective character actively prepared for something coming later, in the midst of something happening now?

Is this an opportunity to explore the theme? Can your characters' priorities reflect real-world beliefs?

Use this prompt for character arc.
  Use this prompt for relationships.
  Use this prompt for plot.

"I wouldn't say that"

One of the easiest ways to differentiate your characters is by their voice, by their diction: the words that they choose to use, the way they string along sentences. And this can reflect how their brains work differently, how they approach ideas and how they put these ideas together.

What would happen in your current or next scene if two different characters said the same idea with completely different terms?

Can this help you explore your theme? Can a difference in wording show differences in socioeconomic positions reflected in the real world? Can you parse out the nuance of a difficult topic by showing subtle differences in diction?

Use this prompt for relationships.
  Use this prompt for world building.

"Hooked on a feeling"

Oftentimes as writers, when we are describing feelings, the difficulty of the description or the depth of the feeling to the character determines how much time and how many words we spent describing that feeling. If it's really tough to describe a feeling, it can take more words, it can really hit the character harder, we're going to take more words. However, whatever we take the most words to do is what the reader will take as most important to them.

What would happen in your current, next, or last scene, if you expanded the feelings of the main or perspective character that you as the writer think is the most important for the reader to understand. Unpack those feelings so that it took more words in any other feelings you described in the scene.

Is this a way to draw attention or explore the theme for your reader? Can you unpack and draw attention to feelings directly related to your theme?

Use this prompt for character arc.

"Mirrored failure"

A big obstacle when writing a book is making sure that your main character is staying active. Passive characters can be unrelatable and cause the reader to dislike them or lose interest in your story. You can really bog your whole book down. Some traps that can cause passive characters are flashbacks, observing, and long descriptions. If they're not directly related to an active scene or an action, such traps can slow reader momentum or even bore them into putting the story down.

What would happen in your current or next scene if your main or perspective character remembered a time they acted and failed as it related to an action in the present scene?

Can this failure directly relate to the big idea of your book's theme? Can the two juxtaposing moments in time dig into the details of opposing beliefs of your theme? Can the thoughts of the character reflecting on that failure speak explicitly to your own position on the theme's topic?

Use this prompt for character arc.

<u>Use this prompt for plot.</u>
<u>Use this prompt for world building.</u>

"Forget it"

I don't know about you, but I'm always forgetting stuff. I know I'm old, but like, there's just too much stuff to remember in life.

What would happen in your current or next scene if, while your characters were actively doing something, you reminded the reader of something that that character was forgetting?

Can this dramatic irony produce comedy? Is this a way to reinforce your theme? Can your character unwittingly make a mistake that underlines your perspective of the topic the theme tackles?

Use this prompt for character arc.
  Use this prompt for relationships.
  Use this prompt for plot.

"You don't understand"

W hether we are neurotypical or neurodivergent, it's not always easy to communicate what we are thinking to other people. It's very difficult to get somebody to see through our own perspective, no matter how good we are with words, no matter how well we know the other person, no matter how well we understand the social cues that we share with our audience.

What would happen in your current or next scene if your main or perspective character was having a difficult time explaining a thought to another character and had to keep changing tactics?

Can this inability to communicate be a metaphor for the story's theme? Can the multiple explanations of the character cover multiple approaches to the story theme?

Use this prompt for character arc.
  Use this prompt for relationships.
  Use this prompt for plot.
  Use this prompt for world building.

"You can't do that"

Satisfying character arcs are the ones that finish with the main character doing something that seemed absolutely impossible for them to do. And I'm not talking about a superhuman feat. I'm talking about something that internally, you wouldn't think that the character was capable of because of trauma or emotions. They come to admit that they needed help, or for them to trust someone else.

What would happen in your current or next scene if your main or perspective character alluded to not being able to do the one thing that you know that they're going to have to do in the climax? If you just reinforced that there's no way that this character is going to be able to do that?

Can you use this to underline the theme? Can the task either be a metaphor for the theme, or an example of the theme in micro or macrocosm? Can the cause of the character's inability to perform the task be a way to illustrate the theme?

Use this prompt for character arcs.
  Use this prompt for plot.

"What's changed?"

Oftentimes as we get older, we learn more context about the world around us and understand things more. We can see the same piece of information, memory, or object and understand it better. We have learned, we have grown, we just get the context more than we did the first time that we encountered it.

What would happen in your current or next scene if your main or perspective character revisited a memory, an object, or an idea with a new context and realized that there is an added meaning or a different meaning entirely?

Is this a way to underline your theme? Can the character's new understanding of allude to your understanding of the theme?

Use this prompt for character arc.
  Use this prompt for world building.

"What if it's wrong?"

As we get older, we find out that a lot of the things that we learned or were taught are wrong. There are fables, there's mis- education, there's propaganda. There are also just things that we pick up here and there that we take as fact and internalize while they're just false.

What would happen in your current or next scene if your main or perspective character discovered that a long-held belief was wrong?

Can the widely-held belief be a metaphor for something in real life? Can the discovery of the misinformation represent to the author understanding the truth of the theme?

Use this prompt for character arc.
　Use this prompt for relationships.
　Use this prompt for world building.

"Try and try again"

"The definition of insanity is trying the same course of action and expecting different results." This is a quote that is vaguely attributed to Albert Einstein even though there are no actual primary sources that say Einstein said this. If anyone has ever practiced any physical sport such as weight training or distance running, you understand that it's simply not true. Truth is, we often reset and try the exact same course of action over and over again and we constantly get different results. In fact, I would say if you're writing a story and your character isn't trying the same course of action multiple times, it might not be believable.

What would happen in your current or next scene if your main or perspective character was trying the same course of action multiple times and they were surprised by the results?

Can the struggle of the attempts say something about your theme? Can the repeated course of action represent something in real life? Can the nuance of the theme somehow get unpacked in the series of attempts?

Use this prompt for character arc.
  Use this prompt for relationships.
  Use this prompt for plot.
  Use this prompt for world building.

"Why it won't work"

This prompt is something that I use throughout the writing process, during drafting, throughout revisions and once I get notes back from other people. Oftentimes, we're in our own heads about what to do next, especially when a character is planning their next step, or in the middle of doing something to achieve their goal. And there are things that they cannot do for certain reasons, because it doesn't make sense to the character or because it doesn't make sense for the setting.

What would happen in your current or next scene if your main or perspective character, thought through something that wouldn't work, and thought it through either in dialogue or in their head.

Is this a way to show your reader that you've thought of all possible angles of your position on the theme? Can you dissect aspects of the theme indirectly?

Use this prompt for character arc.
  Use this prompt for relationships.

Use this prompt for plot.

"You changed"

Everybody changes, especially characters in a story. And sometimes in real life, when we see how others have changed, it can affect us. We can be proud, ashamed, or even jealous.

What would happen in your current or next scene if your main or perspective character sensed a change in another character?

Can this change be tied to the theme? Can you use the change in this character to make a point about your position on the theme's topic? Is the change a direct reference or indirect metaphor for the theme?

Use this prompt for character arc.
   Use this prompt for relationships.
   Use this prompt for plot.
   Use this prompt for world building.

"Moving goalposts"

O ne of the character arcs that I absolutely love reading is, not only does the character change throughout the story, but they realize that their goa at the beginning of the story is not the same as what they want by the end of the story.

It shows growth, it shows perspective, a lot of time and like while you are at middle grade, it shows that they're growing up.

What would happen in your current or next scene if your main or perspective character started to doubt that they actually wanted their goal?

Is this an opportunity to explore the writer's theme? Can the shift in the character's thinking mimic how you came to your own conclusions about the story's theme?

Use this prompt for character arc.

"The downside"

There are very few plans or ideas that are beneficial to every single party involved. Once you really think about a possible plan and the repercussions, oftentimes you will figure out that there is at least one party or person who is not going to benefit. Someone is going to end up with the short end of the stick.

What would happen in your current or next scene if your main or perspective character realized that someone would not benefit from the ultimate goal? And specifically, someone would be hurt by that goal.

Is this a way to show nuance in the theme? Or is the revelation of who experiences harm a metaphor for the theme? Can the realization of harm reflect how you solidified your own stance on the theme in real life?

Use this prompt for character arc and world building.

"Not the theme"

One of my favorite aspects of a story is the theme, the idea or a question that the author is exploring throughout the story. Very seldom is the theme actually stated within the book. Usually, it is tangential to the main character arc, or even the main character objective. It's the idea that you as the author are exploring; a "What if" or deeper truth that is within the story.

What would happen in your current or next scene if your main or perspective character incorrectly stated the theme? Either said something close to the theme or just got it completely wrong.

Can the character arc explore your theme? Will this lead your reader to understand the point you're making about the theme? Will the reader more easily compare the thought process of the character to their own?

<u>Use this prompt for character arc.</u>

"Reveal"

Sometimes I find out that people that I've worked with, known for years, or have become close with are gay. Because gay people exist. Queer people, gay, lesbian, trans, ace, aro people just exist. Their existence doesn't hve to be the point of a story or move the plot along. Nor do they need to come out or specify the nuance of their gender.

What would happen in your current or next scene if a character let another character know that they're gay?

Is this a way for you as an author to use your words to fight bigotry? Can the added realism of diverse sexual identities make your theme more accessible to real-world comparison?

Use this prompt for relationships.
  Use this prompt for world building.

Index: Glossary of Terms

Backstory: The history of your characters or world. Stuff that happened before the story starts, like the villain's traumatic past or the time the main character painted their room.

Call to Adventure: This is like the hero's invitation to join along with or embark on the story. It's the moment they're given a challenge or a problem to solve.

Character flaw: Nobody's perfect, right? Well, neither are your characters. These are the quirks or issues that make them more human and relatable. Maybe the hero is consistently brave except for a fear of spiders? As opposed to an obstacle, a character flaw will not change throughout the story. The flaw won't be fixed or defeated.

Character arc: the character's roller coaster of internal change. A character arc is their journey from starting out one way and changing or evolving as the story goes on. It's like watching them go from "I can't do this" to "I totally can do this!" Arcs can concern a character's intelligence, maturity, emotional intelligence, wisdom, or morality.

Character journey: This is the series of events your character experiences through the story. It's not just about the physical travel; it's about the emotional beats they go through internally along the way.

Draft Zero: Halfway between an outline and a rough draft. It can contain snippets of dialogue or description, but without scenes or chapters completely fleshed out.

Dramatic (or literary) Irony: The gap of knowledge between a reader and characters. When the audience is in on a secret that the characters don't know about. Like watching a horror movie and shouting, "Don't go in there!"

Failure: An unsuccessful attempt. Very necessary to the character's arc. A setback obstructing a goal that they can internalize and grow from. Failure isn't bad in a book – it is necessity to make the story more interesting and show how they overcome challenges.

Goal: Everyone's got something they want, right? Well, characters are no different. A goal is a wish or what they're striving for. They can be small for a scene, or overarching for the duration of a story.

Hook: A distilled phrase or sentence that encompasses the most interesting aspect of a story or book.

Info-dump: When information is revealed to the reader in an inorganic way. Whether in dialogue or a character's thoughts, an unnatural recalling of the circumstances of the character and world. When you shove a ton of information at the reader all at once, which can be overwhelming.

Juxtapose: To compare side-by-side.

Magic system (or tech): Fantastical elements which are the differences between the real world and the world of the story.

Main Character: The character who leads the story, whose actions further the plot toward the climax.

Metaphor: Describing something indirectly through a comparison, but saying one thing is literally another. You know when you say something's "a piece of cake" but you're not actually talking about dessert? That's a metaphor – using something familiar to describe something else in a creative way.

Mood: It's like the vibe of a story or scene. Is it spooky, joyful, or tense? Mood sets the emotional tone for the reader.

Perspective Character: Think of this character as the one holding the camera. They're the lens through which the reader sees the story. You're basically stepping into their shoes.

"Show, don't tell": Common advice to writers to take the reader through actions in order to fill out an idea, rather than describing the idea. Rather than saying "Lydia was sad," show Lydia crying into her ice cream.

Story Seed: Any starting point from which to think up an entire story. This can be a moment in the story, a character, a bit of dialogue, the plot, the world, or almost any initial idea for an entire tale.

Tension: At its core, tension is the chain of questions that keeps a reader interested. Usually summed up as "what happens next," it is a worry or fascination the writer gives the reader to drive them forward in the story. It's the feeling that something is about to happen. Tension's like the "dun dun dun" music in a thriller movie.

Theme: This is the big idea or message hiding behind your story. It's like the life lesson your characters and readers might learn along the way.

Try/Fail cycle: Remember when you tried to ride your bike without training wheels and fell a bunch of times before finally getting it? That's the try/fail cycle – characters facing challenges, failing, learning, and trying again.

Unreliable narrator: When the person relaying the story can't be completely believed or trusted. Someone who might not be giving you the whole truth.

World building: The given circumstances within a story; the rules, the history, the geography – everything that makes your fictional world the way it is..

Index: Priming the Idea Machine

D o you need a story seed? Then I've got your first prompt right here: I call it the idea machine.

All machines need a form of priming– a way to get the fuel into the mechanism in order for the machine to start and run. This exercise has the goal of generating ten to fifteen new story ideas by priming it with two pre-existing story ideas.

Gather your writing tools: You'll need pen and paper or a laptop and set a 15-minute timer.

Begin with two unoriginal ideas: These can be ideas from existing books, movies, or stories that you're familiar with. I'll use *Battle Royale* and *Annihilation*.

Write these two ideas down in a simple form, just to express the hook: "Hunger Games as a competition between middle schoolers with guns" and "What if area 51 caused people to go insane?"

Use this momentum to continue to write story ideas in a hook format. Write down ten or more original ideas of your own. These could be new characters, settings, or plot concepts.

Aim for at least ten more ideas, and if you're really inspired, you might even come up with 15 or more.

This exercise is an effective way to kick start your imagination when looking for fresh story ideas. It encourages writers to boil down big story concepts to distilled hooks, building upon existing concepts to create something new and unique.

About the Author

Zack Jeffries has written several books under several pen names (not to mention plays and screenplays). As Zachary Jeffries, he's authored Young Adult Fantasy novels like The Unseen Curse, Angel of Fate, and Witches of Fate. As Z Jeffries, he's authored Middle Grade Science Fiction, such as The Hide & Seek Chronicles and Pro Wrestling Saves Earth. Jeffries lives in the American Midwest with his family and dog. He appreciates cheese.

www.ingramcontent.com/pod-product-compliance
Lightning Source LLC
Chambersburg PA
CBHW011220120626
46545CB00010B/3077